Clarence Bloomfield Moore

Certain aboriginal Remains of the Alabama River

Clarence Bloomfield Moore

Certain aboriginal Remains of the Alabama River

ISBN/EAN: 9783337232535

Printed in Europe, USA, Canada, Australia, Japan

Cover: Foto ©ninafisch / pixelio.de

More available books at **www.hansebooks.com**

CERTAIN

ABORIGINAL REMAINS

OF THE

ALABAMA RIVER.

BY

CLARENCE B. MOORE.

REPRINT FROM THE JOURNAL OF THE ACADEMY OF NATURAL
SCIENCES OF PHILADELPHIA, VOLUME XI.
PHILADELPHIA, 1899.

PHILADELPHIA
P. C. STOCKHAUSEN,
No. 55 N. 7th ST.
1899.

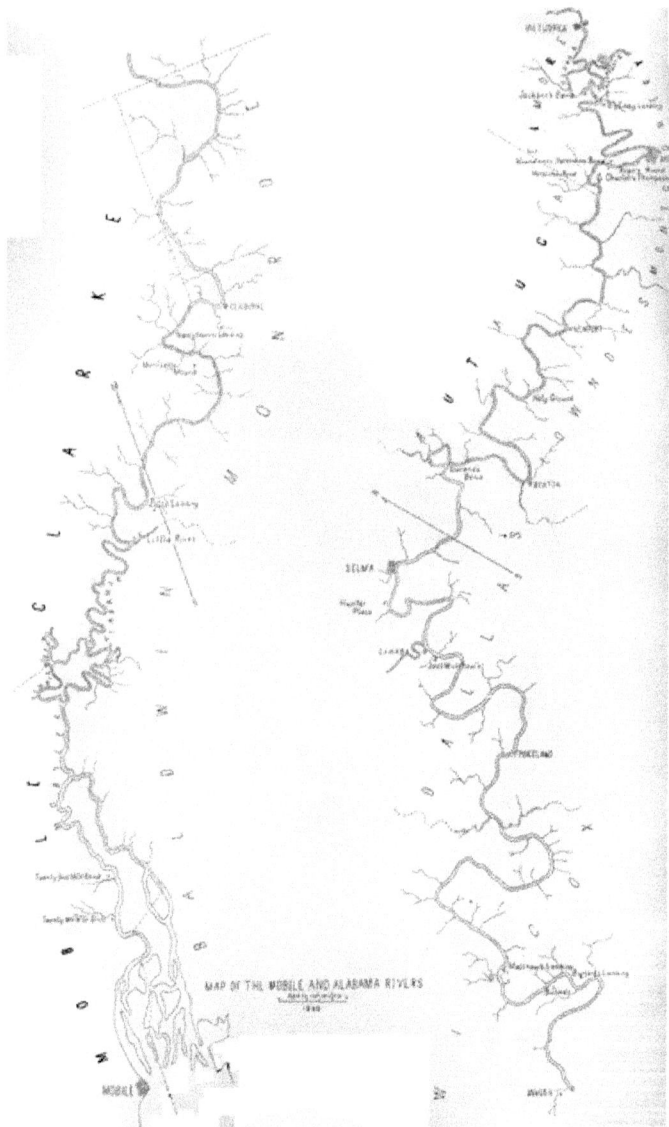

MAP OF THE MOBILE AND ALABAMA RIVERS

CERTAIN ABORIGINAL REMAINS OF THE ALABAMA RIVER.

By Clarence B. Moore.

The union of the Coosa and Tallapoosa rivers, in the central part of the State of Alabama, forms the Alabama river, which, running in a westerly, and then in a southerly, course through the State, about 375 miles by water, is joined by the Tombigbee river and thence on, under the name of the Mobile river, continues a distance of 50 miles, by water, to Mobile bay, a part of the Gulf of Mexico.

The Mobile and Alabama rivers are navigable by flat-bottomed steamers of light draft between Mobile, at the head of Mobile bay, and Montgomery, about 400 miles farther up, and in high water even beyond the "Forks," though for years Montgomery has been the terminus for the regular line of steamers.

This Report treats of certain aboriginal remains bordering the Mobile and Alabama rivers.[1]

The time devoted by us in person to the location and investigation of the aboriginal remains of these rivers was about three months of the early part of 1899, during which time a great number of landings were visited, and at important ones conversation was had with persons familiar with the territory for miles around.

In addition, Mr. L. D. Cutting, engineer of our boat for years and thoroughly familiar with mounds, twice went from Mobile to Selma on the regular steamers in the busy season, making inquiries at landings and of passengers, and also visited Montgomery in prosecution of the search.

Furthermore, a resident of Montgomery, familiar with the river, accompanied by a companion, was employed by us to go down the river in an open boat from Montgomery to Matthews' Landing, about 200 miles by water, making inquiries along the way.

Although the attention given by us to the Mobile and Alabama rivers does not compare with that accorded by us to the St. Johns river, Florida, and to the Georgia coast, yet it was fully ample to indicate that mounds along these rivers were of rare occurrence and, as a rule, insignificant in size. It must not be supposed, however, that the meagre list of aboriginal remains investigated includes all located by us and by those working in our interests. While the majority of owners of property along the river hastened to give cordial permission to investigate, a number ignored our communications, though several times addressed. However, the aboriginal remains investigated were presumably representative.

[1] The map is mainly taken from the Government report, as are the distances, which are by water, "Annual Report of the Chief of Engineers," 1884, Ex. Doc 1, Pt. 2, Vol. 2.

The Mobile river, running mainly through swamps, could have offered few sites for aboriginal abode; but the banks of the Alabama, though swampy in places, often rise into lofty bluffs, and on them might be expected mounds far exceeding in number those which seem to be present. In many places pebbles, chips of stone, sherds, arrowpoints, mussel-shells, indicating dwelling sites, strew the surface, and we think it likely that, as mounds are so often wanting near such sites, the people who lived there buried rather in cemeteries, which, unmarked above the surface, have escaped notice.

But even allowing for many places of sepulture not located by us, it is not likely the borders of the Mobile and Alabama rivers were as thickly settled as were those of Florida's greatest river. The shad which visit the St. Johns, the bass so abundant in its clear waters, are wanting in the Mobile and Alabama rivers. In the great Florida stream, shell-fish were so abundant that shell-heaps covering acres remain along the banks, some a score of feet in thickness. Along the Mobile are shell-heaps of insignificant size, while on the Alabama scattered shells only mark former places of abode. But even apart from these considerations, it must be borne in mind that the Mobile and lower Alabama run largely through swampy ground, malarial in summer, a fact which aborigines choosing a place of abode would doubtless take into consideration. Yet we are told[1] that De Soto found the Mobilian Indians living along the banks of the Alabama, between the present sites of Montgomery and Mobile, and later, remnants of the Mobilians dwelt near the coast; bands of Alabamas were settled from the union of the Coosa and Tallapoosa to below where Montgomery now stands; Creeks and Choctaws occupied other portions of the river. Still these Indians had villages on elevated points, doubtless avoiding the swamps, and did not line the banks as did the Indians of the St. Johns.

No systematic investigation of the Mobile and Alabama rivers has been made previous to our own. In the Annual Report of the Bureau of Ethnology[2] we find brief notices of investigation conducted at two points on the Alabama river, one of which is not definitely located; but beyond this we believe excavations have been limited to ignorant search for treasure or to the spasmodic digging of the seeker after relics.

Aboriginal Remains Investigated.

Mound near Twenty-One-Mile Bluff, Mobile county (Mobile river).
Mound near Twenty-Four-Mile Bend, Mobile county (Mobile river).
Mound near Little river, Monroe county.
Mound near Potts' Landing, Monroe county.
Morrisette Mound, Clarke county.
Cemetery at Nancy Harris Landing, Monroe county.
Mound near Webb's Landing, Wilcox county.
Mound near Burford's Landing, Wilcox county.

[1] "The History of Alabama," Pickett. Reprinted 1896.
[2] 1890-91, page 289-296.

Mound on Burford Place, Wilcox county.

Mounds near Matthews' Landing, Wilcox county (4).

Mound on Joel Matthews' Place, Dallas county.

Mound on Hunter Place, Dallas county.

Cemetery at Durand's Bend, Dallas county.

Mounds on Charlotte Thompson Place, Montgomery county (4).

Mound on Rogers Place, Montgomery county.

Mound near Horseshoe Bend, Elmore county.

Mounds in Thirty Acre Field, Montgomery county (2).

Mound in Big Eddy Field, Montgomery county.

Mound at Jackson's Bend, Elmore county.

MOUND AT TWENTY-ONE-MILE BLUFF, MOBILE COUNTY (MOBILE RIVER).

Twenty-one miles above Mobile is one of the few spots of high ground on the low-lying banks of the Mobile river. About three hundred yards west of the landing, close to the road, was an unstratified mound of clay, 6.5 feet high and having a basal diameter of 58 feet. A large trench had previously been dug into the center through the southern part of the mound. The remainder of the mound was investigated by us with the kind consent of Mr. George R. Dupree of Mobile, resulting in the discovery of parts of two disturbed skeletons. No pits or graves were found. Loose in the clay were numerous sherds, mainly undecorated; the bottom of a small vessel with four feet; three stone hones; one chert arrowhead; one smoothing stone; three large glass beads.

MOUND NEAR TWENTY-FOUR-MILE BEND, MOBILE COUNTY (MOBILE RIVER).

About three-quarters of a mile in a westerly direction from the landing at Twenty-Four-Mile Bend, in a cultivated field, is a low, irregular mound much ploughed down, the property of Mrs. Smith, reported to be a Choctaw Indian of almost pure blood.

The mound, which is of sand with a large admixture of clay, has been dug through by a former owner in a vain search for treasure.

A small amount of digging done by us was without result.

MOUND NEAR LITTLE RIVER, MONROE COUNTY.

Little river enters the Alabama about one hundred miles above Mobile.

In a cultivated field, about one-half mile from the mouth of Little river, on the left-hand side, going up, was a mound long ploughed over and consequently much extended. When investigated by us its height was about 2 feet. Its original diameter of base probably did not exceed 50 feet. The mound was dug through by us with the cordial permission of Mr. T. S. Moore, of Tensaw, Ala., the owner.

There was no evidence of previous investigation, though sherds of excellent ware and interesting decoration, evidently from burial urns, scattered over the surface, told of wreckage wrought by the plough.

The mound was a mixture of clay and sand without stratification. Bits of charcoal and other evidence of fire were present throughout.

The burials remaining were largely central or near the center. A number had been disturbed by the plough and doubtless many more had been taken from the mound in former time by the same agency. Such as remained were of the bunched variety [1] with three exceptions. One of the bunches had six femurs of adults with two skulls and other bones of adults, and at one side the skull and certain bones of an infant.

A skeleton was extended in anatomical order from the pelvis down. Below it was a skull with a few ribs. Nearby was another skull.

Just below the surface, crushed to small pieces, were parts of the remains of one or more vessels. Among them lay the bones of an infant.

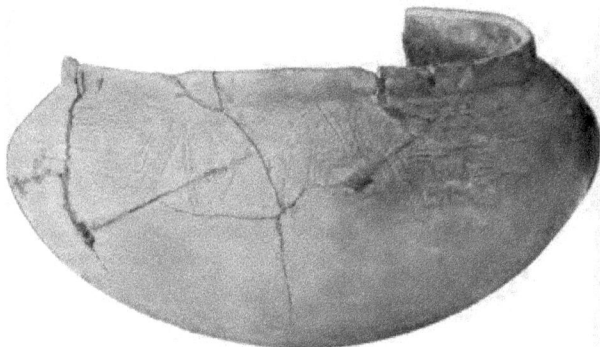

Fig. 1.—Earthenware vessel. Mound near Little river. (About four-ninths size.)

Almost in the center of the mound were many fragments of two vessels crushed by the plough and wanting certain parts, doubtless ploughed away. The remaining portions have been reunited and are, with nearly all the collections made by us, at the Academy of Natural Sciences of Philadelphia.

The under vessel, B, contained the bones of an infant. The ware was of fairly good quality, without admixture of pounded shell. Height, 6.5 inches; maximum diameter, 13.7 inches; diameter of aperture, 10.7 inches. The vessel is semi-globular in shape, with a small upright rim decorated with notches around the exterior edge. The body bears a complicated incised decoration partly shown in Fig. 1.

[1] For forms of burial see our "Certain Aboriginal Mounds of the Georgia Coast," pg. 6 et seq. Journ. Acad. Nat. Sci., Vol. XI.

Vessel B had been capped by Vessel A, a handsome circular dish of excellent ware without admixture of shell, black in color, thick and highly smoothed. The edge of the rim is decorated with notches and its interior surface with incised, parallel lines at intervals. Below the rim, on the inside, is incised cross-hatched decoration. Diameter, 16 inches; depth, 4.5 inches (Fig. 2).

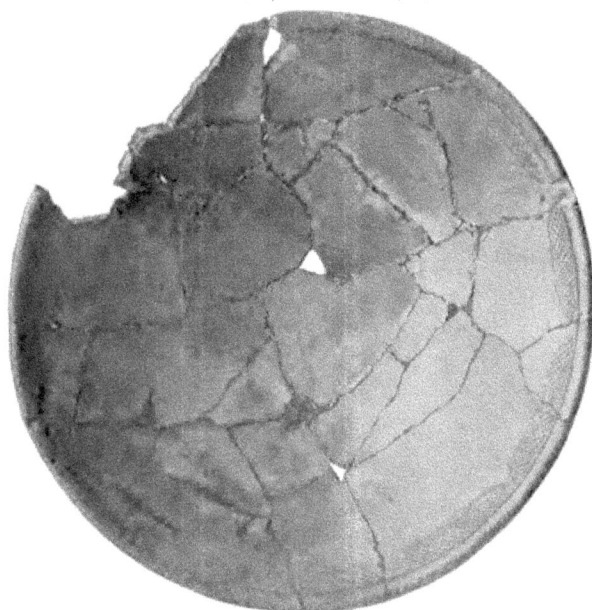

Fig. 2.—Vessel A. Mound near Little river. (Three-eighths size.)

With a burial, near the head, were: a neat lance-head of quartz, a small vessel of inferior ware, irreparably broken into fragments, and a pair of ear-plugs somewhat decayed and broken. Each ear-plug has been made of two discs of shell, each somewhat over one inch in diameter. Each pair of discs has been joined together by a sort of mortar composed of calcined shell, pulverized, and clay.[1]

[1] Determined by Mr. S. H. Hamilton of the Academy of Natural Sciences of Philadelphia.

We shall have occasion later in the Report to refer at greater length to earplugs of this type.

In caved earth was a rude vessel with pointed projections around the outside of the rim. Height, 2.7 inches; maximum diameter, 4 inches (Fig. 3).

Fig. 3.—Vessel of earthenware. Mound near Little river. (Full size.)

A head of a predatory bird, modelled in red earthenware, blackened exteriorly, which doubtless had seen service as the handle of a vessel, lay loose in the earth. Part of the bill is missing (Fig. 4).

Also in loose earth was a disc of earthenware, cut from a sherd. In former Reports we have had occasion to mention these discs which doubtless were used in games. They occurred in great numbers in some of the mounds of the Alabama river, and their presence has been noted from South Georgia to Canada. Curiously enough they are almost, if not entirely, absent from the

Fig. 4.—Earthenware head of bird. Mound near Little river. (Full size.)

Florida mounds investigated by us, which is likewise the case as to the discoidal stone. They are referred to in Mr. Stewart Culin's exhaustive "Chess and Playing Cards." [1]

Three discoidal stones were in caved earth or were thrown back by the diggers in the mound. A handsome one, probably of clay-stone colored with iron, is 2

[1] "Report of the U. S. National Museum," for 1896.

inches in diameter and 1 inch in thickness. Another is of the same size, while the third has a diameter of 3.5 inches, a thickness of 1.5 inches. These two are of a close-grained volcanic rock, the larger being probably porphyry.[1]

With the large bunched burial, to which we have already referred, were: two undecorated, circular gorgets of shell, both badly broken; six massive shell beads, finely preserved; numerous glass beads; one small sheet copper bead; one perforated pearl, the only one met with by us in Alabama, though the chroniclers of De Soto speak of their great abundance there; one pair of earplugs and a single one, the mate to which was doubtless overlooked by us, all of the type referred to before; two shell pins in fragments, of the ordinary type, made of the columella of a marine univalve cut down for the shank with the original diameter left for the head. With all these were three handsome shell pins differing from the usual type, aptly described by Professor Holmes[2] as follows: "They differ from the pins heretofore described, being in all cases unsymmetrical. The shaft is flat and somewhat curved and joins the mushroom-shaped head near one edge. This results from the peculiar shape of the portion of the shell from which the pin is derived . . . ."

Such pins have the shaft cut from the parietal wall of the shell and the head from parts extending to either side of the suture, as shown in Fig. 5.

Fig. 5.—Dagger showing part from which the pin is made. (Not to scale.)

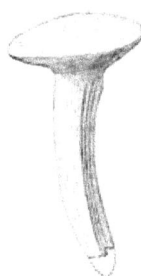

Fig. 6.—Shell pin. Mound near Little river. (Full size.)

The three pins are about equal in size, each being about 2.5 inches long with diameter of head of 1.5 inches. One is shown in Fig. 6.

All shell pins found by us have been near the skull; therefore, we believe them to have been used as ornaments in the hair.

[1] All identifications of rock in this Report have been made by Dr. E. Goldsmith, of the Academy of Natural Sciences of Philadelphia. As we have not furnished microscopical slides from the specimens, exact determination has been impossible.

[2] "Art in Shell of the Ancient Americans." Second Annual Report of the Bureau of Ethnology, page 216, Fig. 8, Pl. XXX.

Near the surface, together, were : the iron or steel blade of a knife, two gun flints, vermilion paint and a brass object presumably belonging to a musket or rifle.

In this mound was an intrusive burial which had been made in a large pine box fastened with hand-made nails. With the skeleton were two brass buttons.

MOUND NEAR POTTS LANDING, MONROE COUNTY.

This mound, the property of Dr. G. G. Scott, of Mt. Pleasant, Ala., who kindly consented to its investigation, is about one mile in a southerly direction from Potts' Landing.

The mound, in a cultivated field, ploughed over for a long period, is much spread out and very irregular in shape. Its height at present is 5 feet 7 inches; its basal maximum and minimum diameters are 118 feet and 100 feet, respectively.

The central part of the mound, dug out by us, showed the material to be a mixture of clay and sand. There were no indications of use as a burial ground.

MORRISETTE MOUND, CLARKE COUNTY.

This mound, not far from Marshall's Bluff Landing, in a cultivated field, is about 8 feet high and 40 feet across the base, approximately. Untouched by the plough, owing to the steepness of its sides, it is the most symmetrical mound met with by us on the Alabama river, almost a perfect truncated cone in shape.

The owner, Mr. Robert Morrisette of Perdue Hill, did not reply to our request for permission to investigate. We refer to the mound here only in the idea that it richly deserves a systematic investigation, permission for which might be obtained should there at any time be a change of ownership.

CEMETERY AT NANCY HARRIS LANDING, MONROE COUNTY.

The neighborhood of this landing suffered greatly by the freshet of 1886 which wrought such havoc along the banks of the Alabama.

In conversation with persons living along the river and with colored people resident at the landing, we heard of pots, broken and whole, of tobacco pipes and of human bones, washed up by the flood and left scattered over the surface on the subsidence of the water.

A careful examination was made by us and sounding rods were used in all likely-looking territory, unfortunately without material success, though scattered human bones, fragments of pottery and, in one case, the earthenware head of a bird, which had served as the handle for a vessel, were met with.

The territory around the landing is of clay covered with sand. This sand, in nearly every instance, had been swept away with the burials it contained, leaving, we fear, little chance for future archæological work in this vicinity.

MOUND NEAR WEBB'S LANDING, WILCOX COUNTY.

The mound, showing no mark of cultivation, was in a ploughed field on the flat summit of a small hill, about three quarters of a mile in a northwesterly direction from the landing.

The mound, which was dug down with the kind permission of Mr. M. L. Stabler, of Peach Tree, Ala., had a height of 4 feet; a basal diameter of 38 feet. A small hole had previously been dug into the center of the mound which was of sand with slight admixture of clay.

Human remains, very badly decayed, were met with at seven points and were represented by a skull here, a skull with a single long bone there, and the like. Once the crowns of teeth alone remained.

With one burial was a beautifully wrought celt, probably of greenstone, 9.7 inches in length, measuring across its evenly ground blade 2.5 inches, gracefully tapering at the other end to a rounded point .4 of an inch in diameter.

Near another burial, one on the other, were two small, rude, undecorated gorgets of shell, roughly circular.

Several arrowheads were loose in the earth.

Mound near Burford's Landing, Wilcox County.

Our thanks are due to Mr. W. P. Murphy, of Rockwest, P. O., for permission to investigate this mound, which is situated in woods which apparently have grown on ground previously cleared, about 1.5 miles in a southerly direction from Burford's Landing. The height of the mound was 6 feet 8 inches; across the base it was 58 feet. The only previous examination apparent was a small, shallow hole near the summit.

A large trench made by us showed the mound to be of sand. With the exception of fragments of decaying bones, several arrowheads and two rough knives of stone, nothing was met with.

Mound on Burford's Plantation, Wilcox County.

This plantation is on the left-hand side of the river going up, about one-half mile below Holly Ferry. The mound is about one mile W. S. W. from the landing, in the heart of a swamp. It had been much trampled by cattle and consequently spread out and reduced in height, which, at the time of the investigation, was 5 feet. The diameter of base was about 45 feet. It was thoroughly investigated with the cordial permission of Mr. W. P. Burford, of Rockwest P. O., Ala., and proved to be of rich clayey sand.

At several points were decayed remains of parts of skeletons. Two arrowpoints lay loose in the sand.

Mounds near Matthews' Landing, Wilcox County (I).

About 1.5 miles in a southwesterly direction from the landing, in a ploughed field, about 400 yards from the river, was a mound much ploughed down and irregular in shape. Two great depressions nearby showed whence the material was derived.

The present height of the mound is 5 feet 4 inches; the major and minor axes of its base are 120 feet and 70 feet, respectively.

It was investigated by kind permission of Messrs. Miller and Bonner, of Camden, Ala., through whose courtesy all our work near Matthews' Landing was done.

Extensive trenching of the mound, which was of clay covered with sand, showed it to have been of a domiciliary character with no yield beyond sherds, one perforated mussel shell and one earthenware "checker."

About 50 yards in a southwesterly direction from the mound just described, near the river bank, with the plantation road passing over it, was an irregular undulation from 1 to 2 feet in height. Its exact area was impossible to determine though it was considerably less than that of the neighboring mound. A large portion was dug through by us. The upper stratum was of clay 4 or 5 inches thick. Next came a layer of yellow sand 18 inches to 2 feet in thickness, having a slight admixture of clay, while the bottom layer, from 1 to 2 feet thick, was of clay blackened with charcoal and organic matter and containing many sherds. In it were a large number of pottery "checkers" and one small one of shell, also the earthenware head of a duck, formerly the handle of a vessel. The ware was of good quality, containing an admixture of pounded shell, while some was black and highly polished.

Burials were met with at two points: one being the bunched remains of an adult and of a child; the other, also of an adult and of a child, had the bones in anatomical order.

The crania, badly broken, showed artificial flattening. The Choctaws, we are told,[1] compressed the skulls during infancy, and hence were called "flatheads" by the traders. Probably other Indians along the Alabama practised this same custom of cranial compression.

This mound had every appearance of having been a dwelling site like its neighbor, with burials, perhaps of a later period than the mound itself.

About 400 yards in a W. S. W. direction from the landing is a mound on undulating country, with probably an average height of 7 feet. The sides, washed by the river in times of unusual flood, probably originally ran steeply up to a perfectly level plateau, most likely intended for domiciliary purposes. Pine trees, some 2 feet in diameter, are on the mound which bears no appearance of previous cultivation. The mound at present has somewhat the shape of a blunt wedge, probably conferred by wash of water and, doubtless, formerly was rectangular in shape like other mounds of its class. The summit plateau, in an easterly and westerly direction, has a diameter of about 158 feet, with a base diameter about 35 feet greater. Across the western portion of the plateau, the thick end of the wedge, the diameter is about 100 feet, the base-diameter about 45 feet in excess.

Various trenches and pits indicated the mound to have been made of sandy clay, with a superficial layer of sand, of varying depth, say from 1 to 3 feet. About 3 feet down, extending through the mound on the same level, was a thin layer of earth blackened probably by fire and admixture of organic matter, seemingly indicating a long-continued period of occupation. No interments were found

[1] Pickett, quoting Adair, "History of Alabama," page 125 et seq.

below this layer, though some lay on it, from which we concluded that the original mound had been increased 3 feet in height and subsequently used for burials.

About three-fourths of the plateau was dug through by us to a depth of 3 feet, resulting in the discovery of burials as follows:

Burial No. 1.—With its top 9 inches below the surface, was a vessel (Fig. 7) of coarse ware, consisting of clay with admixture of pounded shell. The body, which is semiglobular, is undecorated; the neck is upright and surrounded with perpendicular ridges; the rim is flaring. A good example of this type, Vessel BB, is shown in our account of the aboriginal cemetery at Durand's Bend.

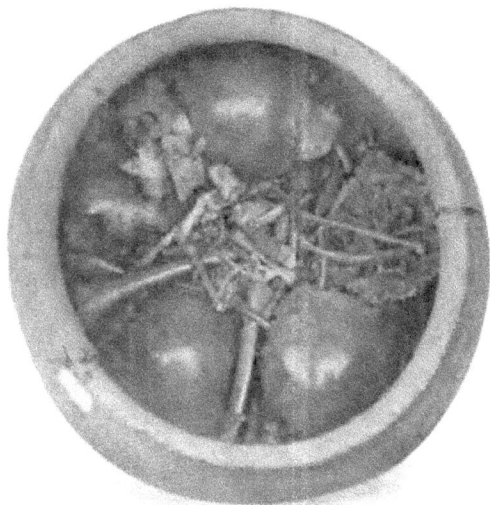

Fig. 7.—Vessel containing skeletons of infants. Mound at Matthews Landing. (About one-third size.)

The vessel has a height of 8.5 inches; a maximum diameter of 11.5 inches; a diameter at the mouth of 12 inches.

Ranged around the sides were disconnected parts of skulls of several infants, having beneath them and partly around them many other bones, probably the remainder of the skeletons which had been disarticulated and carefully packed away

With these, occupying a central position, was the skeleton of a very young infant which had been buried in anatomical order. All these bones have been kept exactly as found, and now, soaked with glue and coated with shellac to impart solidity, occupy their original position, a certain amount of earth which had entered through a crack having been removed. The arrangement of the bones is well shown in Fig. 7.

Over Vessel A, inverted, was a circular, undecorated dish of very coarse ware—clay and pounded shell—having a maximum depth of 3 inches and a diameter of 13.5 inches. In this dish is a large crack, dating from early times, as is shown by a perforation in either side through which had been passed a cord or sinew to lash the parts together, after the aboriginal fashion.

On top of the upturned base of the dish (B) were a number of fragments of earthenware which had formed part of another vessel, doubtless put on for additional protection.

We have here a form of burial new to our work, namely plural burial of skeletons in a single urn. Along the Georgia coast we found urn-burials of single skeletons and urns filled with cremated remains of various individuals. Later in this report we shall see a repetition of this plural form occuring in the aboriginal cemetery at Durand's Bend.

Burial No. 2.—2 feet below the surface was the skull of an adult in fragments, as were all crania found unenclosed in this mound. No other bones were in association. With the skull was an undecorated vessel with globular body and upright neck. Height, 3.75 inches; diameter of body, 3.5 inches. With this vessel was a diminutive bowl, 1.9 inches in diameter, 1 inch in height. This little toy had incised decoration over the entire exterior surface (Fig. 8).

Fig. 8.—Earthenware vessel. Mound at Matthews' Landing. (Full size.)

Such vessels are usually supposed to have been placed with children. In the skull, which this little bowl accompanied, the wisdom teeth were present. With the other objects was a little bowl 1.7 inches long, 1.5 inches broad, .75 inch deep wrought from a pebble, which, possibly, to a certain extent, had been hollowed out by nature.

Burial No. 3.—A bunched burial consisting of certain bones of a child, without the skull, lay 18 inches below the surface. This burial was surmounted by part of a bowl, crushed, from which the rim was missing.

Burial No. 4.—13 inches down were parts of skeletons of an adult and of a child, mingled. Alongside was part of an undecorated vessel of about one quart capacity. It will be noted that the canny aborigines who built this mound, as in other sections of the country, were sometimes inclined to be quit of tributes to the dead by interment of objects otherwise useless. Still, their gifts to the departed compare favorably with those of the present time.

Burial No. 5.—Fragments of a skull in caved earth.

Burial No. 6.—Certain bones of an adult, without cranium, 5 feet down.

Burial No. 7.—15 feet down, upright, was a vessel of about two quarts capacity, with semi-globular body and flaring rim decorated with knobs around the outer margin of the mouth. This vessel, badly broken by blows from a spade, contained certain bones of a young child, namely: one-half of a lower jaw, one clavicle, certain ribs, pelvic bones, and one piece of a vertebra. With these bones was an undecorated, imperforate ornament of shell, a trapezoid in shape, 2 inches long with an average breadth of 1.5 inches. Beneath the vessel were certain bones of an adult.

Burial No. 8.—A bunched burial consisting of a cranium with a few bones, all apparently belonging to one person, 2 feet below the surface.

Burial No. 9.—A bunch consisting of twelve tibiæ, thirteen femurs and other long bones, 51 inches down. Scattered among these bones were fragments of earthenware representing part of a vessel.

Burial No. 10.—A few scattered fragments of bone just beneath the surface.

Burial No. 11.—A large, inverted vessel with rude line and punctate decoration lay over the skull of a child, which surmounted a number of its bones heaped together. This vessel, broken in small pieces by roots and pressure, was sent to the Peabody Museum, Cambridge, Mass., as were the bones which, soaked in glue and allowed to dry in place, are preserved, as to position, exactly as found.

Burial No. 12.—This burial consisted of one-half of the lower jaw, some ribs and a clavicle with the cranium to one side, all belonging to an adult. In association were two shell beads each about .5 of an inch in diameter.

Burial No. 13.—2 feet down was a bunched burial consisting of one humerus, bones of both forearms, two femurs, two tibiæ, one fibula.

Burial No. 14.—Isolated skull of an adult, 20 inches down. With it was a discoidal stone of ferruginous claystone, 1.8 inches in diameter. On the major, or lower, surface, are cut two concentric circles (Fig. 9). Somewhat farther in the mound, on the same plane, were pairs of femurs, humeri, tibiæ, radii, ulnæ, all parallel to each other with a cranium to one side and above.

Burial No. 15.—On the same plane as Burial No. 14 and 1 foot north of it, was a bunch of adult long bones, all parallel. Just beyond was the skull of an infant with a few bits of decayed bone.

Fig. 9.—Discoidal stone. Mound at Matthews Landing. (Full size.)

Burial No. 16.—Certain crushed and decayed bones of an infant, including the cranium, lay 15 inches below the surface. With the skull was an undecorated, imperforate disc of shell, 3 inches in diameter.

Burial No. 17.—Two femurs, one tibia, one fibula, one humerus, the cranium, all belonging to an adult, 29 inches down. All these were surmounted by two fragments of a large vessel.

Burial No. 18.—Just under the surface was a bunch of certain bones of an adult and of an infant, mingled.   No crania were present.

Burial No. 19.—Two crania of adults with one of a child.   With these, 30 inches down, were a few bones belonging to at least two adults.

Burial No. 20.—26 inches down, a few fragments of crushed and decayed bones.

Burial No. 21.—45 inches down, a bunched burial of a skull and a few long bones of a child.

Burial No. 22.—Isolated skull of adult, 2 feet down.

Burial No. 23.—A few bits of decayed bone belonging to a child, 1 foot below the surface.

The high percentage of interments of children in this mound is worthy of remark.

Mound on the Joel Matthews' Place, Dallas County.

This estate, about one mile below Cahaba, on the right side of the river going down, had a mound in a large cultivated field, about 40 yards from the woods. Investigation was made with the courteous permission of Mr. B. F. Ellis, of Orrville, Ala., the lessee of the property.

As near as we could judge, the mound, before the cultivation it had undergone, had been about 32 feet across the base.   Its height above the general level was 4 feet 3 inches, though, at the center, a burial lay 5 feet 6 inches from the surface.

The mound was about three-quarters dug through by us, including the entire central portion.   It was of dark brown, loamy sand without stratification.

Human remains, encountered at twenty-one points, consisted of small bunches of human bones and sometimes a single skull.   In no case was a skeleton present or had there been any attempt to bury in anatomical order.   In one instance there was a small deposit of fragments of charred and calcined bones, the only instance of cremation met with by us on the Mobile or Alabama rivers.

No artifacts were present with the burials, and the sole yield from the mound was a few rude arrowpoints.

Mound on the Hunter Place, Dallas County.

The Hunter Place, on the right-hand side of the river going down, is about four miles from Selma by land.

About 500 yards from the landing, on the edge of a cultivated field, was a mound about 50 feet across the base and 7 feet in height.   Its sides were too steep to permit cultivation.   Unfortunately, a narrow trench running N. and S. had been dug completely through the mound.   We are indebted to Mrs. Fanny Pollard, one of the Hunter heirs, residing on the estate, for permission to dig.

Owing to the previous disturbance a complete investigation was not attempted. The eastern part of the mound was mostly dug through by us and a small portion of the western part.

The mound was composed of a mass of clay covered to a depth of several feet with sand.

Human remains, a bunched burial, were met with but once.

In the debris thrown out by previous diggers was a spool-shaped ornament of copper of the pattern often found in Ohio mounds, and a sheet copper disc 2.5 inches in diameter with a central repoussé boss having in the middle a perforation for attachment.

ABORIGINAL CEMETERY, DURAND'S BEND, DALLAS COUNTY.

Durand's Bend, formed by a long curve of the Alabama river, is about thirteen miles above Selma by water. At one point the land is only about 150 yards across, and there, during the great flood of 1886, when the territory was under water, the river cut through in several places, washing away superficial portions. On the subsidence of the flood it was found that parts of an aboriginal burial place had been laid bare and that human bones, earthenware vessels, whole and in fragments,

Fig. 19.

and various other objects of aboriginal make, were scattered over the surface. Many persons from Selma visited the ground, reaping a rich harvest, we were told, and since then others visiting the spot, have located, by the aid of iron rods, numerous vessels under the surface, which they dug up and carried away.

Dr. W. J. Stoddard, of Selma, the owner of the property, a gentleman greatly interested in scientific matters, determined to end reckless digging by unauthorized persons and, for a considerable period, has withheld permission to dig. We are indebted to Doctor Stoddard for cordially placing his entire plantation at our disposal with fullest permission to investigate to any extent we saw fit.

Over six days were spent by us at Durand's Bend, having a considerable number of colored men living on the place in addition to the trained workers from our steamer, some of whom have been with us for years.

Fig. 11.

The territory in which urn-burials were found by us was a cultivated field of about three acres, almost on the river bank and its immediate vicinity. The

Fig. 12.

Fig. 13.

Fig. 14.

Figs. 13, 14, 15, 16. Fragments of earthenware vessels. Cemetery, Durand's Bend. (Full size.)

discovery of vessels elsewhere on the place was reported by colored people living there, but none was found by us though a really exhaustive search was made and much territory, in addition to the field we have referred to, gone over by lines of men prodding at short intervals with iron rods.

The surface of the field and some of the other territory was covered with broken pebbles, chips of stone and numerous sherds. Some of these, evidently from burial urns broken by the flood or by previous visitors, are shown in Figs. 10, 11, 12, 13, 14.

Other sherds were undecorated, or had the check stamp and probably belonged to cooking utensils. Among all these were a few bearing the complicated stamp so familiar in Georgia and Carolina.

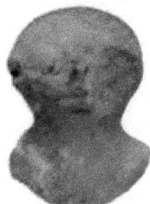

Fig. 15.—Head of earthenware. Cemetery at Durand's Bend. (Full size.)

Fig. 16.—Perforated pebbles. Cemetery at Durand's Bend. (Full size.)

In addition, scattered over the field, were: arrowpoints of quartz; smaller ones usually of black chert; hammer-stones, discoidal stones made from flat pebbles pecked into shape; many discs made from fragments of pottery; a human head in earthenware, about 2 inches high, somewhat injured on one side (Fig. 15); fragments of various implements and a number of pebbles, some clayey and soft, others of a silicious character and hard, each having a perforation, seem-

Fig. 17.—Notched pebble. Cemetery. Durand's Bend. (Full size.)

ingly artificial, though in no case was the perforation of that even character such as was made by the tubular drill used with sand by the aborigines to cut resistant rocks. The holes, on the contrary, were irregular in shape, some showing a certain polish as to the interior surface. These pebbles were not found associated with the dead, but singly and loose in the earth.

Professor Putnam declares them to be natural formations. It is not even likely they were utilized by the aborigines since, as we have said, they lay apart from burials. Certain of these formations are shown in Fig. 16.

During trenching of part of the field and the excavation of vessels many objects, similar to some of those enumerated, were met with and it is probable that those on the surface were left there by the subsiding water.

During our excavation we met with a discoidal stone of *Felsite*, highly polished, a flat pebble notched for suspension (Fig. 17); two canine teeth of large carnivores, one grooved at the base for suspension; an interesting little chisel made from a flat pebble of silicious rock colored with iron, with the beginning of a perforation (Fig. 18), about 2.2 inches long and 1.75 inches across the blade.

Fig. 18.—Chisel of silicious rock Cemetery at Durand's Bend. (Full size.)

Fig. 19.—Pendant of earthenware. Cemetery at Durand's Bend. (Full size.)

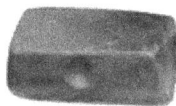

Fig. 20.—"Bannerstone" of hematite. Cemetery at Durand's Bend. (Full size.)

From colored inhabitants we got a small pendant of earthenware with a single perforation (Fig. 19), and a "bannerstone" of polished hematite with an uncompleted perforation (Figs. 20, 21).

Fig. 21.—Cross-section of Fig. 20.

As iron rods, as a rule, located only urns, numbers of trenches were dug, always over 2 feet in depth, through the sand into undisturbed material beneath. This resulted in the discovery of twenty-seven unenclosed burials from 2 to 3 feet below the surface. Two of these were bunched burials; one, a burial of part of a skeleton, mainly in order; one, part of a skeleton, disturbed by a burial beneath; one, a child on its back with its thighs drawn up; one, also a child, on its left side. Twenty-one skeletons lay extended at full length on the back, all but three with arms parallel to the trunk. In one instance the right arm crossed the lumbar vertebræ; in another, the right hand lay upon the pelvis. A child had both hands raised to the shoulders.

The skeletons had no uniformity of direction, but headed to all points of the compass.

Sixteen were of adults, seven were of adolescents or of children. The skeletons probably had been interred when denuded of flesh, though still fairly well connected by ligaments. This was evidenced in a number of cases where bones were wanting, or were placed in improper order or turned in the wrong direction.

Crania were so badly decayed, crushed or penetrated by roots that but two were preserved. These two, found near together, close to the bluff, belonged to singularly well-preserved skeletons. One, of a male (Collection Academy of Natural Sciences, No. 2,168) seems to partake strongly of the negro type. Its companion, however (Collection Academy of Natural Sciences, No. 2,169), shows marked artificial flattening. Adair tells us that the Choctaws practised flattening of the skull. These skulls may belong to comparatively recent interments.

Inhumation of artifacts with unenclosed dead was met with but once at Durand's Bend. Two feet from the surface, extended on its back, was the skeleton of a delicately formed man or of a woman. The bones of the feet were missing, except one heel bone which lay against the pelvis. Near the hand and forearm were eight tines cut from stag horn. They were neither grooved nor perforated, but, nevertheless, doubtless formed part of a wristlet and were attached together by a partial insertion through some material.

Near the chest of the skeleton were a number of small imperforate shell discs, and across the chest, near the chin, was a so-called "hoe-shaped implement" of volcanic rock, 5.5 inches in length, and 4.5 inches in maximum breadth across the blade. As usual with these "implements" it had a countersunk perforation in the shank.

Objects of this type are by no means common. In all our mound work we had met with them but twice before, one in a mound near Blue Creek, Lake county, Florida; another in a mound near Lake Bluff, on the Altamaha river, Georgia. Later, the reader may see that this type was fairly abundant in mounds near Montgomery, where several imperforate specimens were found, as well as certain ones having perforations and one with a perforation begun, but not completed. It may be as well to say here, since we are on the subject of the "hoe-shaped implement," that we do not believe it to have been used as a hoe. All specimens found by us and those found by others, which we have examined, have the edge finely ground and without notch or chipping, which would not be the case had they seen service as hoes. Besides, farther up the Alabama river we found part of a so-called "hoe-shaped implement" made from the soft blue clay found along the banks of the Alabama. Such an object could never have been intended for active use. Furthermore, the shanks of several of the implements found by us show by a discoloration where there has been a handle, allowing a portion of the shank to project behind. The perforation comes along the margin and was doubtless used, where it was present, to lash the handle more firmly. We are convinced that the "hoe-shaped implement" was a ceremonial axe.

No fractures, and in one case only, an osteitis, was a pathological condition present in the bones. The skeletons showed less muscular markings than we have met with in other sections.

A considerable number of urn-burials were met with by us at Durand's Bend, consisting usually of a vessel holding the remains, capped by another, inverted, to keep out the earth. As a rule, the up-turned base of the upper vessel was about 6 inches from the surface, though doubtless before the freshet swept across the bend, the depth was considerably greater.

But the mortuary vessels, so far as noted, are made of a mixture of clay and pounded shells. In shape and decoration they present no marked variety, but for that matter, at the present day, we can hardly boast of a great diversity of type in mortuary receptacles. The under vessel was usually of the type found by us at Matthews' Landing, with the same undecorated body and often with similar perpen-

circular ridges around the neck beneath the flaring rim, or with loop-like handles in place of ridges. This under vessel was usually surmounted by a bowl with little flare to the rim and with incised and punctate decoration. Sometimes the decoration was exclusively on the inside of the neck and rim. At times, however, there had been utilized as a surmounting vessel the body of a vessel of the type ordinarily used as a receptacle and placed beneath. In such cases the rim and neck were missing and presumably a broken vessel had been utilized.

When not otherwise specified in the description, the vessels are imperforate as to the base. The reader may recall that in Florida many, and along the Georgia coast some, vessels were found by us from the bottoms of which pieces had been broken, possibly to "kill" the vessel to permit its soul to accompany the spirit of its master to the happy hunting-grounds; or perhaps, in the case of mortuary urns, to allow the soul to escape. It is interesting to note on the Alabama river the occasional occurrence of this curious custom.

It will be noted that no cremated remains, so abundant among the urn-burials of Georgia or parts of Georgia, were met with by us in the cemetery at Durand's Bend.

FIG. 22.—Vessel A. Cemetery, Durand's Bend. (Three-sevenths size.)

Nearly all the vessels, when discovered by us, were more or less cracked and the cracks, as the vessel dried and contracted, tended to widen. Moreover, many vessels, through long exposure to moisture, were soft and friable. In every case we dug carefully around the vessels and, brushing the earth from them, permitted them to harden in the sun, at the same time applying a quick-setting cement between the margins of the cracks. Before lifting, when the state of the vessels required it, stout cotton bandages tightened by improvised tourniquets were adjusted with advantage, and these bandages were allowed to remain in place until the vessels had made their journey North. In certain cases where vessels, crushed into small fragments, had had principal parts irrecoverably carried away by the plough, and the remaining parts bore no decoration of interest, they were abandoned.

We shall now give in detail a description of the vessels and their contents. All measurements are approximate. The vessels, when not otherwise specified, may be seen at the Academy of Natural Sciences, Philadelphia.

Vessels A and B.—Vessel B, of the type already referred to as coming from Matthews' Landing, which we shall hereafter, for convenience, call the receptacle type, has beneath the rim on the outside, instead of the upright ridges, four small loop-shaped handles, such as are shown on the figure of vessel EE. Its maximum diameter of body is 14 inches; its height, 10 inches. The rim is badly shattered and parts are missing. In B were splinters of decaying bones, one humerus of a very young infant and a mussel shell (*Unio crassidens*).

Vessel B was capped by an inverted bowl (A) with incised and punctate decoration as shown in Fig. 22. Maximum diameter of body, 14 inches; height, 7 inches. In the base was a perforation which could not have come from the metal rods in use for sounding, as the splintering showed a blow from the inside and, moreover, the piece was missing. This is the first case in any section of the country where we have found a surmounting vessel with basal perforation.

Vessel C.—A short distance below the base of Vessel B, to one side, was a bowl (C) intact, with incised and punctate decoration, practically the same as that on Vessel A, having a maximum diameter of 7 inches, a height of 8.5 inches.

It lay inverted about 4 inches above a skull belonging to the skeleton of an infant, in anatomical order.

Vessel D.—This vessel, similar in shape and decoration to Vessel B, was badly broken. It contained a few fragments of bones of an infant and a mussel shell of the kind found in Vessel B. Vessel D was surmounted by fragments of what had probably been a part of a vessel. These fragments, with Vessel D, were sent to Peabody Museum, Cambridge, Mass.

Vessels E and F.—Vessel E, of the usual receptacle type, 11.7 inches high, 17.2 inches in maximum diameter, contained the bones of an infant, with a shell bead, a perforated cockle-shell (*Cardium*) and a small oval, undecorated shell gorget with double perforation. Vessel F was capped by Vessel E, inverted, from which the rim had been broken prior to its burial. The body has a maximum diameter of 18 inches; the height of the fragment is 8 inches. These vessels were sent to the University of Pennsylvania, Philadelphia.

Vessels G and H.—Vessel H, 23 inches across the body and 16 inches in height, of the receptacle type as to shape, with the ridges and, in addition, six small loops beneath the margin, contained parts of the skeleton of an adult, namely: two shoulder blades, two collar bones, breast bone, twenty-four ribs, the pelvic bones and nineteen vertebræ. The shoulder blades and corresponding vertebrae were in anatomical order. The skull and all bones of the extremities, except those of the feet, were wanting. These bones were in fairly good condition, and it is impossible to ascribe the absence of the other bones of the skeleton to decay. The bones filled but a small portion of the vessel, so the interment of but part of a skeleton was not necessitated.

Surmounting and partly covering Vessel H was an inverted vessel (G), without rim, of the type of Vessel E.

Vessels I and J.—Vessel J, of the receptacle type, 15 inches through the body at its maximum and 11.8 inches high, contained the bones of an infant, apparently

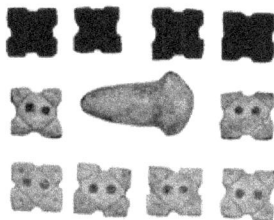

Fig. 23.—Beads and ornaments of shell. Cemetery at Durand's Bend. (Full size.)

in anatomical order, though exact determination was difficult owing to disarrangement caused by removal of infiltrated sand. Near the neck was a stopper-shaped ornament of shell, 1.25 inches long and presumably a necklace made up of forty-four rectangular pieces of shell, incised and doubly perforated, all closely resembling one another. Certain of these beads, with the ornament, are shown in Fig. 23.

Turned over the mouth of Vessel J was a bowl (I), 12.2 inches maximum diameter and 5.5 inches in height. Its decoration is incised and punctate (Fig. 24). It has two small perforations made by the sounding rod.

Fig. 24.—Vessel I. Cemetery Durand's Bend. (One-half size.)

These two vessels lay among mingled fragments of two other vessels with scattered bones of an infant. Presumably the fragments represented an earlier burial broken by the introduction of the later one.

Vessels K and L.—Vessel K, of the regular receptacle type, has a maximum diameter of 20 inches; its height is 14 inches. It contained certain bones belonging to the skeleton of an adult: the vertebræ and ribs, beginning with the fifth dorsal vertebra, down; the shoulder blades; the collar bones; the pelvic bones; the breast bone and the bones of both feet. Here again we have a fragmentary burial not necessitated by a limited size of vessel. In the mound in Dumoussay's Field, Sapelo Island, Ga., we found the upper part of the skeleton of a woman, buried in a vessel of earthenware with the lower part buried beneath. In this case, however, the vessel was packed to its full capacity, which was far from being the case with Vessel K.

Over the bones, on the base of Vessel K and wholly contained in it, was part of an inverted bowl, the rim from which was entirely missing.

Vessel M.—This vessel, of the usual receptacle type, was badly broken and deficient in certain parts which doubtless had been ploughed away. It contained a few decaying bones of the skeleton of an infant. On the fragments of this vessel lay a mass of small pieces of a dish, once, no doubt, a surmounting vessel. This urn-burial was discarded.

Vessel N.—This vessel, just under the surface, had lost its upper portion and the surmounting vessel by exposure to the plough. The vessel differed from others at Durand's Bend. It had been of fine, light-yellow ware with incised scroll work painted a brilliant red. On the base were a few bits of decaying bones of an infant.

Vessels O and P.—Vessel P, of the receptacle type, with loop handles in place of ridges, fell into small pieces upon removal. It contained a few bones of an infant.

An inverted bowl (O) had been let into Vessel P for a short distance. This bowl, with slightly flaring rim with incised decoration on the inside, has a maximum diameter of 12.75 inches, a height of 5.2 inches.

Vessels Q and R.—Vessel R, of the receptacle type, contained the bones of an infant, seemingly in anatomical order. It has a height of 13 inches; a maximum diameter of 19 inches. There is an aboriginal perforation in the base.

Over Vessel R was an inverted vessel (Q) without a rim, which fell into small pieces upon removal.

Vessels S and T.—Vessel S, of the usual type, having loops beneath the margin, has a maximum diameter of 20 inches; a height of 14 inches. On the base were certain bones of a skeleton belonging to a period toward the close of infancy. These bones were not in regular order, and the skull, except the lower jaw, was wanting. Above the bones, which were lying on the base of the vessel, had been placed a sort of circular dish (T), inverted, having a maximum diameter of 13.5 inches and 2.8 inches deep. This dish bore no decoration with the exception of certain notches around the margin. While most of the bones were covered by the dish, a part of the margin lay against a scapula which was upright and

FIG. 25.—Vessel V, containing burial—Cemetery, Durand's Bend—(One-half size.)

parallel to the side of the larger vessel, and certain bones lay beyond that part of the base of Vessel S included beneath the inverted dish.

Vessels U and V.—Vessel V, the usual type as to shape, with loops instead of ridges around the neck, one of which was missing, is 22 inches in maximum diameter and 15 inches high. It contained one of the most striking burials which it has been our fortune to meet with. As a general rule, cracks in the receptacle vessel or the crushing in of the surmounting one permits the entrance of earth; thus covering the contents of the burial-urn and making difficult their uncovering without disarrangement. In this case, however, Vessel U, of the receptacle type but without rim, had kept out all foreign matter, except a slight deposit of earth on

FIG. 26.—Vessel W. Cemetery, Durand's Bend. (Six-thirteenths size.)

the burial beneath, so the greater vessel, when uncovered, was seen to be filled to the level of the rim with bones presumably belonging to two skeletons; the smaller ones at the bottom, then layer upon layer of the major long bones, capped by two skulls side by side, looking toward the South. One cranium was of an adult male. The other, of an adolescent, seemed to indicate artificial antero-posterior compression. Near it were a few shell beads. We did not discover whether other artifacts accompanied the remains since, to keep the bones exactly as found, the entire mass was deluged with glue without removal, to hold the bones in place and impart consistency. Subsequently, certain bones in contact with the sides of the vessel were cemented to it and then the mass received two coats of shellac. Even in this condition, the vessel being somewhat broken and the bones certain to fall apart when jarred, it was deemed impossible to secure safe transportation North, either by freight or by express. Therefore, the vessel with its contents was securely packed in a light box with handles and, by courteous consent of J. C. Morrison, Esq., District Superintendent of the Pullman Palace Car Company, New Orleans, the box was brought North by us in the sleeping car on our return. A good halftone representation of the bones as they appear in the vessel, looking down, is given in Fig. 25.

Vessels W and X.—Vessel X, of the usual receptacle type, having loop handles, is 9.7 inches high and 14.2 inches across at its widest part. It contains a pile of bones probably belonging to two infants whose skulls lie on top. One shell bead was visible among the bones which were not removed but were glued in place.

On Vessel X, the aperture down, was Vessel W, a bowl 13 inches in maximum diameter and 6.5 inches high, having incised and punctate decoration as shown in Fig. 26.

Vessels Y, Z, AA, BB, CC.—These vessels, found as shown in Fig. 27, constitute one of the most interesting urn-burials ever met with by us.

Vessel BB (Fig. 28), of the receptacle type, 17.7 inches in maximum diameter and 12.2 inches in height, contained parts of an infant's skeleton in anatomical order, though the skull and certain other bones were missing. Shell beads were in association.

BB was capped by a vessel (Z), inverted. AA and Y also inverted, the lower part of their rims resting against BB, were placed obliquely, so as nearly to cover Vessel Z.

A small vessel (CC), height, 2.5 inches, diameter of body, 4.5 inches, lay on its end in the earth with part of its rim passing against the lower portion of Vessel BB.

Vessel CC, of very poor material, is in the shape of a bowl with rude incised decoration and handles roughly representing the head and tail of a bird. Portions of the vessel have crumbled away. From the end of bill to tip of tail the diameter is 7 inches.

Vessel AA is a bowl of red ware. Its maximum diameter is 12.8 inches; its height, 6.6 inches. Its somewhat flaring rim has a series of < < incised on its inner surface, making spaces left bare and filled with red coloring matter alternately.

Vessel Z is the counterpart of Vessel AA, with the exception of being 1 inch less in height (Fig. 29).

Vessel Y, with basal perforation, is of the receptacle type, though used as a surmounting vessel. It is 12.5 inches in maximum diameter and 8.6 inches in height. The ornamentation differs from the usual upright or loop handles, as is shown in Fig. 30.

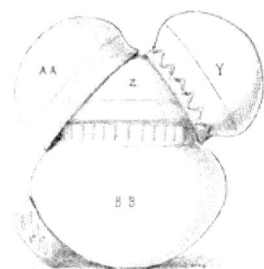

Fig. 27.—Urn-burial, drawn from sketch made on the spot. Cemetery, Durant's Bend. (One-ninth size.)

Fig. 28.—Vessel DD. Cemetery, Durand's Bend. (About one-third size.)

Fig. 29. Vessel E. Cemetery, Durand's Bend. (About one-half size.)

Fig. 30.—Vessel Y. Cemetery Durand's Bend. (About one-half size.)

Vessels DD and EE.—Vessel EE, the usual receptacle type, badly broken, had on the base decaying bones of an infant, with an undecorated, circular shell gorget, 1.7 inches in diameter, having a double perforation.

Fig. 31.—Vessel DD. Cemetery, Durand's Bend. (About five-sevenths size.)

Covering the aperture of Vessel EE, was an inverted bowl (DD), with incised and punctate decoration, 14.3 inches across at its broadest part and 6.8 inches in height (Fig. 31).

A hole had been knocked in the base of Vessel DD, and over this hole had been placed, inverted, the base of another vessel, presumably to keep out the earth.

This urn-burial complete was sent to the Peabody Museum, Cambridge, Mass., where broken portions have been pieced together. This burial, as it appeared when found, is shown in Fig. 32.

Vessels FF and GG.—These vessels had been crushed and shattered into small pieces, among which were shell beads and fragments of bones of an infant.

Fig. 32.—Vessel EE surmounted by Vessel DD in position as found.   Cemetery, Durand's Bend.   (About three-fourteenths size.)

Vessels HH and II.—These were crushed to small pieces and parts had been carried away by the plough.   The remaining fragments, among which were a few decaying bones of an infant, were abandoned.

Vessels JJ and KK.—In all respects similar to the preceding ones.

Vessels LL and MM.—These were the smallest mortuary vessels met with by us at Durand's Bend. The under one (MM) has a maximum diameter of 9.5 inches. It is 6 inches high.   It is of the usual type and contains the skull of an infant and some, perhaps all, of the skeleton which was not in anatomical order. These bones, in better condition than infant remains usually are, were hardened by us by means of glue and are preserved intact in the urn.

Inverted over the mouth of Vessel MM was a bowl (LL) in fragments, with flaring rim decorated on the inner surface with rudely incised lines. Parts of Vessel LL, recovered and glued together, showed the bowl to have had a maximum diameter of 10 inches; a height of 3.7 inches.

Several additional vessels, found in small fragments, will not be particularly described.

Just beneath the surface, with no human remains in association, was a vessel, heart shaped in section and decorated as shown in Fig. 33.

Its maximum diameter is 4.5 inches; its height, 1.8 inches. It unfortunately received a blow from a spade.

Two small undecorated pots lay near the surface apart from human remains, while another, with rude incised decoration, came from the vicinity of a broken urn. This vessel is of the coil method of manufacture where coils of clay are superimposed in manner much as we make a straw hat, and of all the vessels found, so far as noted, contained no admixture of pounded shell.

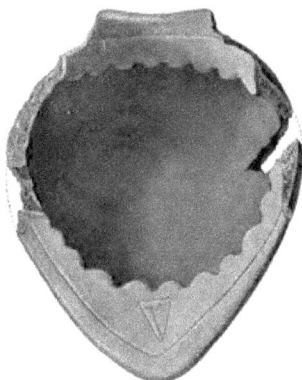

Fig. 33.—Earthenware vessel. Cemetery, Durnal's Bend. (Full size.)

MOUNDS ON THE CHARLOTTE THOMPSON PLACE, MONTGOMERY COUNTY (4).

About six miles below Montgomery, on the left side of the river, going down, in a cultivated field, about one-quarter mile from the water, was a mound 67 feet through the base, approximately, with a summit plateau having a diameter of about 32 feet. The height of the mound was about 9 feet though its position across a natural ridge made its altitude appear somewhat greater on two sides.

Though the mound was uninjured by cultivation, unfortunately a trench 10 feet to 12 feet broad had been dug from the margin into the summit plateau some distance though stopping short of the center of the mound.

The mound was investigated by us, with the kind permission of Mr. W. G. Henderson, of Montgomery, the owner.

Beginning at the margin, a trench 20 feet across was run below the base of the mound to the margin of the summit plateau. No burials were met with outside of 15 feet of the margin of the plateau. On the discovery of human remains at that point the trench was widened to include the entire plateau and 15 feet beyond on either side. This trench was continued through the mound until it was apparent no farther burials lay beyond. In this way a mere shell was left standing, in which, presumably, there are few, if any, interments.

Four or five feet in from the margin of the mound, whose outer portion was of sand, there began a nucleus of clay around and over which the mound was built. The clay rose sharply and speedily attained the height of about 3 feet, which it maintained with slight variation throughout. This flat table of clay was, as we have said, surrounded and surmounted by sand.

Human remains were found in the sand, in the clay, and, in a few cases, in pits extending below the level of the mound. An earnest attempt was made to keep score of the burials, but skeletons in anatomical order (flexed and partly flexed) were comparatively few, while bunched burials, interments of parts of skeletons and bones scattered in all directions, were so numerous and so intermingled that the task was given up as hopeless.

There were no cases of cremation, though in several instances thin layers of what seemed to be charcoal lay above the bones.

This mound was, to us, in one respect of peculiar interest, for, from top to bottom, were objects of iron, of glass, and of other material, derived from the whites, which proved the mound to be of post-Columbian origin and emphasized what has always been our contention, that in a mound built after contact with Europeans, artifacts obtained from them will be amply in evidence.

SHELL.

Pins.—Shell pins were present in great numbers. Indeed it seemed as though every third burial was provided with them. In one case four lay with a single skull. Excluding numbers of decayed pins and others broken in excavation, no less than ninety pins, from 1.5 inches to 7 inches in length, were recovered from the mound. Among these were four of the interesting variety described by us as coming from the mound near Little river.

Gorgets.—Twenty-seven shell gorgets, irregularly circular, from 1.8 inches to 4.9 inches in diameter, lay with burials, usually those of children—one child having two. Unfortunately, none bore engraved decoration, though nine had a circle of semi-perforations on one side near the margin and four were marginally decorated with notches (Figs. 34, 35).

Certain gorgets had a single perforation for suspension, while some were doubly and even trebly perforated. In several cases where holes had worn through, others had been drilled.

Beads.—Shell beads were with the burials in bewildering profusion and variety, some no larger than a good-sized pin's head, others, great sections of axes of marine univalves, 1.6 inches in length.

A few flat beads with incised decoration and doubly perforated, somewhat resembling those from Durand's Bend, were present (Fig. 36).

With two burials were numbers of small marine univalves (*Marginella*) perforated for stringing.

FIG. 24.—Shell gorget. Mound on Charlotte Thompson Place. (Full size.)

Ear plugs.—As is well known, it was the custom of many of our aborigines to pierce the lobe of the ear and to enlarge the opening so that various objects, some of considerable size, could be worn by thrusting them through the lobe. This curious

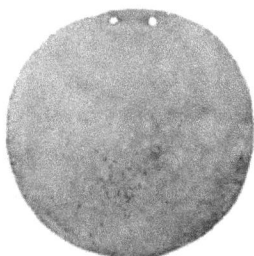

FIG. 25.—Shell gorget. Mound on Charlotte Thompson Place. (Full size.)

FIG. 26.—Shell beads. Mound on Charlotte Thompson Place. (Full size.)

custom, still to a certain extent kept up by women, which attained its maximum as to size of perforation in Peru, permitted the buttoning in of various objects, some of copper, such as are found in Ohio and elsewhere, or of stone, copper-coated, like those taken by us from Mt. Royal, Florida, or of shell, of the type referred to by us as coming from the mound near Little river. In the mound on the Charlotte Thompson Place were three pairs of shell ear-plugs, each pair taken from near a cranium, and several fragmentary ones decayed and broken. One pair was of the type found in the Little river mound, that is, discs of shell, one smaller than the other, fastened together with a mortar made of clay and pounded calcined shell. In one respect this pair of ear-plugs differs from those at Little river in that one disc of one ear-plug is centrally perforated. The other two pairs have each ear-plug carved from a solid piece of shell, with one flange, doubtless the one worn on the inside, somewhat smaller than the other. Both pairs are perforated centrally through the minor axis. But one ear-plug is sufficiently well preserved to furnish measurements as to original size. This shows one side to have a diameter of 1.6 inches; the other, 1.4 inches.

Fish-hook.—On the base of the mound, associated with human remains, with bone piercing implements and a bone fish-hook 2.5 inches long, was a neatly made fish-hook of shell, 2.8 inches in length, grooved for attachment of the line. In this instance, though they are of different materials, we shall speak of the fish-hooks together. The shell fish-hook is shown in Fig. 37; the bone one, in Fig. 38.

Fig. 37.—Shell fish-hook, Mound on Charlotte Thompson Place. (Full size.)

Fig. 38.—Bone fish-hook, Mound on Charlotte Thompson Place. (Full size.)

In relation to fish-hooks in North America, Rau, " Prehistoric Fishing," page 122, says, " In the first place I have to allude to their great scarcity in the eastern portion of North America and to state that those which have been found within that area are almost exclusively of bone. They occur more frequently on the Pacific Coast, especially in California latitudes and there they consist of bone or shell." [1]

Professor Rau cites a number of early authors on North America who refer to fish-hooks of bone.

Professor Holmes, "Art in Shell," [2] page 207 *et seq.*, tells us, " The use of shell in the manufacture of fishing implements seems to have been almost unknown among the tribes of the Atlantic Coast and with the exception of a few pendant-like objects, resembling plummets or sinkers of stone, nothing has been obtained from the ancient burial mounds of the Mississippi Valley. Hooks of shell, however, are very plentiful in the ancient burial places of the Pacific Coast. . . ."

[1] "Smithsonian Contributions to Knowledge," 1884.
[2] Second An. Report of Bureau of Ethnology.

Abbott, "Primitive Industry," page 208, figures a bone fish-hook and comments on the rarity of such objects in eastern North America.

C. C. Jones in his "Antiquities of the Southern Indians" points out the absence of fish-hooks from the districts described by him, and in all our mound work in Georgia, in South Carolina, in Alabama and in Florida, where, in addition, shell heaps were exhaustively searched, we have met with fish-hooks in this instance alone, so the reader can appreciate the interest of this discovery, which furnished, so far as we can learn, the only shell fish hook found east of the Pacific Slope.

Scraper.—A fine mussel-shell (*Unio heros*) was found, perforated for attachment to a handle and showing marks of wear at one end.

Drinking Cup.—A marine univalve (*Cassis cameo*), with interior portions cut out to form a drinking cup, lay near a skull. This is the first instance where a drinking cup has been found by us wrought from a shell other than the conch (*Fulgur*).

Shells.—Seven mussel-shells (*Unio heros*) were found near a burial, while another, filled with tines of a stag-horn and decaying piercing implements of bone, lay near human remains.

A cockle-shell (*Cardium magnum*) lay almost in contact with a skull.

EARTHENWARE.

Fig. 39.—Earthenware disc. Mound on Charlotte Thompson Place. (Full size.)

Discs.—A number of discs made from pot-herds, for use in games, lay in midden refuse throughout the mound and a disc of earthenware, slightly broken, having on one side a central depression surrounded by six rays, also was present (Fig. 39).

Vessels.—The yield of earthenware vessels from this mound was disappointing in view of the fact that fragments of good ware were present in the mound. In one instance only were vessels found with the dead. Two bowls lay on

Fig. 40.—Earthenware vessel. Mound on Charlotte Thompson Place. (Full size.)

FIG. 41.—Earthenware vessel. Mound on Charlotte Thompson Place. (Full size.)

the ribs of a skeleton. One, with incised and punctate decoration exteriorly on the rim, has a maximum diameter of 4.8 inches and is 2 inches in depth (Fig. 40). The other, with incised decoration on the interior of the rim, is 4.8 inches in maximum diameter and 1.7 inches deep (Fig. 41).

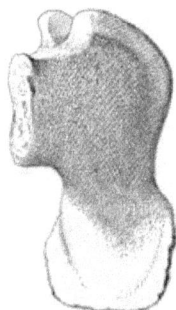

FIG. 43.—Tobacco-pipe of earthenware. Mound on Charlotte Thompson Place. (Full size.)

A handle of a vessel, modelled after an animal-head, was loose in the earth (Fig. 42).

Tobacco-pipes.—The tobacco-pipes, three in number, from this post-Columbian mound, were poor in quality and uninteresting as to design.

FIG. 42.—Handle of earthenware. Mound on Charlotte Thompson Place. (Full size.)

One lay with midden refuse in the margin of the mound (Fig. 43).

Another, somewhat broken, has a handle and a decoration of notches around the margin of the bowl (Fig. 44).

Fig. 44.—Tobacco-pipe of earthenware. Mound on Charlotte Thompson Place. (Full size.)

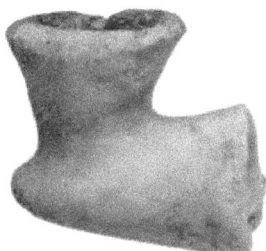

Fig. 45.—Tobacco-pipe of earthenware. Mound on Charlotte Thompson Place. (Full size.)

The third is undecorated (Fig. 45).

The two latter lay with human remains.

Fig. 46.—Stopper-shaped object of earthenware. Mound on Charlotte Thompson Place. (Full size.)

Stopper-shaped Object.—In eaved sand was an object of earthenware resembling a mushroom in shape, having a height of 1.5 inches; a maximum diameter of 2.5 inches. This may have served as a stopper for a water-bottle (Fig. 46).

BONE.

Piercing Implements.—A number of piercing implements of bone of the usual type, often badly decayed and broken, came from the mound; also a bone implement showing oblique wear at one end, the use of which we cannot determine.

Anklet.—At the feet of one skeleton were a number of tines in close association, cut from stag-horn, which had doubtless been attached to an anklet. Similar ones came from near the wrist of a skeleton in the cemetery at Durand's Bend.

Fish-hook.—Reference has been made to this.

STONE.

"Celts"—Excluding broken implements, there came from the mound, nearly always with burials, thirteen hatchets and chisels of the usual rocks, from 3 to 7 inches in length.

"*Hoe-shaped Implements.*"—Always with burials, were three "hoe-shaped implements" or ceremonial axes, as we believe them to be, each perforated through the shank somewhat above the blade and none showing breakage or chipping. Plainly visible on two, were marks where a handle had encircled the shank, leaving part of it projecting behind. The length of each is about 5.5 inches; in breadth of blade they vary between 4.5 and 5.3 inches.

The material in one case is *Granulyte*; in the other two, *Felsite*.

A part of a "hoe-shaped implement" made from the soft blue clay of the bluffs of the Alabama river, lay loose in the earth.

Gorget.—A beautiful gorget of *Felsite*, 2.6 inches long and 2 inches across the blade, is modelled exactly after the "hoe-shaped implement" in shape, though the perforation comes higher on the shank. Its length is but 2.5 inches; its breadth across the blade, 2 inches. Should we consider this a "hoe-shaped implement," it is the smallest on record (Fig. 47). It was found with the bones of an adult.

Discoidal Stones.—Three discoidal stones, handsomely polished, were met with and a number of flat pebbles rounded by chipping.

Miscellaneous.—During the excavation were found several rude arrowheads; a neat little one of black flint; a rude cutting implement of quartz; hammerstones; and a curious little object of silicious rock, 1.4 inches in length, resembling a fiddle bow, seemingly of artificial design (Fig. 48).

FIG. 48.—Unidentified object of stone. Mound on Charlotte Thompson Place. (Full size.)

FIG. 47.—Gorget. Mound on Charlotte Thompson Place. (Full size.)

COPPER.

At all depths in the mound were ornaments of sheet copper, always with interments and often associated with shell, stone, glass or iron. On one side of some was a coarse woven fabric preserved by copper salts.

Pendants.—Eleven pendants of sheet copper in fairly good condition, and a number of fragments of pendants were met with. Nine of these pendants resemble in shape a spearhead with rounded point. One pair of these found together has rude incised decoration uniform in type though differing slightly in detail. In each a part of the conventional aboriginal eye is represented as shown in Fig. 49. The two pendants, which differ slightly in size, are about 4 inches in length and 2 inches in maximum diameter. Like all pendants of this type, each has a single perforation for suspension.

Three of the pendants, somewhat smaller than those described, have a decoration conferred by pressure, including a section of the human eye toward the upper end.

One pendant, with a length of 5.5 inches and a maximum width of 1.5 inches, has no decoration except marginal indentations.

Two other pendants are too much corroded for exact description.

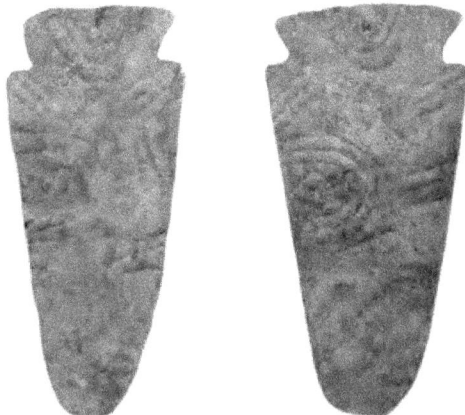

Fig. 49.—Pendants of sheet copper. Mound on Charlotte Thompson Place. (Full size.)

One pendant, about 4 inches long and with a maximum width of 2 inches, is of much more solid material than the others. It is badly corroded. Still clinging to it is a remnant of cord upon which a number of shell beads are strung.

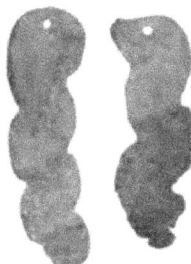

Fig. 50.—Pendants of sheet copper. Mound on Charlotte Thompson Place. (Full size.)

All decoration on the pendants is of purely aboriginal design. We shall describe and illustrate this type more fully in our account of the mounds in the "Thirty-Acre Field."

A pair of sheet copper pendants found end to end extending across the vertex of a cranium, have a wavy outline common to both but not exactly coinciding. The material of one is thicker than that of the other (Fig. 50).

Breast-pieces.—We call by this name oblong plates of sheet copper with two or three holes in the middle, presumably for attachment to garments.

Five such pieces were present in this mound, one somewhat broken by pressure against a bone.

Two, 4 inches by 8 inches, and 5.5 inches by 8.5 inches, respectively, seem to be undecorated. One of these shows distinct lamination, that overlapping of the metal in places through rude hammering processes, which we look for in aboriginal copper.

One breast-piece, 2.8 inches by 8 inches, has a row of marginal indentations and on one side punched decoration which a heavy deposit of carbonate rendered almost indistinguishable when found. This deposit, however, yielded to dilute acid. The plate was submitted to Professor Putnam, who writes as follows :

"The copper band was just received and studied by Willoughby and myself. The following are our conclusions :

"The band is very likely from an officer's belt or perhaps helmet. The small holes about the edge indicate that it was fastened thoroughly to some object for which it was made. The design is that of a spread eagle with a lion on each side facing the eagle. The design was made by a series of punchings with a metal tool (thus - - -). It is not in drawn lines like our native work.

"The design is European and of the heraldic character. I believe you will find some such design on 16th and 17th century objects.

"Is it not likely that some Indians got this and other European things in the mound, from some of the early soldiers or settlers, that this piece was punched in the center and worn by an Indian?"

Of the remaining two pieces, one, 2.2 inches by 6 inches, has for decoration indentations around the margin and transverse rows of indentations. The other, 1.1 inches by 3.2 inches, greatly carbonated, is seemingly without ornamentation. A small fragment of cord still remains in the two perforations.

Upon most of these ornaments fragments of coarse vegetable fibre adhere.

In addition to these was a piece of sheet copper with the two longer sides straight and parallel, and the other two curving outward. Its length is 5.5 inches ; its breadth, 3.5 inches. About .75 of an inch apart, longitudinally, are two raised bosses and apparently other decoration near the margin. The piece is badly carbonated and broken. On the side which lay nearest the skeleton still remain remnants of a comparatively fine fabric, doubtless belonging to a garment. On the outside a coarse, woven vegetable fabric still remains, which probably enveloped the entire skeleton.

Disc.—On the skull of a child, 8 feet 7 inches from the surface, with diminutive shell beads, was a sheet copper disc, .8 inch in diameter, decorated on one side with three concentric circles.

In the second part of our "Certain Sand Mounds of the St. Johns River, Florida " [1] we included a monograph on aboriginal copper as viewed from a chemical standpoint. Our conclusions, we believe, have been universally accepted. As certain of our readers, unfamiliar with the question, may not have access to the work referred to, we venture upon a brief résumé of our conclusions and the way they were arrived at.

Native copper, that is metallic copper found in nature, is of great purity, as pure as, or purer than, can be produced by any smelting processes of the present time. In addition, there is no reliable record of the discovery of lead in native copper.

[1] Journ. Acad. Nat. Sci., Vol. X.

This native copper is present in great quantities near Lake Superior, where aboriginal mines have been discovered; nuggets are found in the "drift" and native copper, to a certain extent, has been found in various States and in Cuba.

In Europe the supply of copper is not obtained from native copper but from ores, almost invariably sulphide ores, which are rich in impurities and contain quantities of arsenic, etc., which even now are hard to eliminate and which, in earlier times, were more than the rude smelting processes of those days could successfully cope with. It is stated that earlier German coins have, in late years, been resmelted with profit to obtain the silver contained in them.

In Europe, furthermore, it was the custom to introduce lead during treatment of the copper ores.

Now, analyses of copper found in aboriginal mounds in which no objects of European provenance are present, show the copper to be of the highest purity and always free from lead.

Therefore, we know that the aborigines of this country made use of native copper. They could not have obtained the metal from the whites, as it is purer than could be smelted today from the sulphide ores of Europe and is far purer than was produced by the comparatively rude processes of the 16th, 17th and 18th centuries.

The reader may see from the foregoing that there should be little difficulty in determining chemically the provenance of copper, provided a careful analysis is made.[1]

In the Charlotte Thompson Mound, which, from top to bottom, contained artifacts of European origin in close association with objects of aboriginal make, a study of the copper is of particular interest.

One of the breast-pieces from the mound had an irregular appearance, showing uneven thickness and marked lamination, the overlapping of parts of the copper upon other parts, which we often see in aboriginal work, being markedly noticeable and particularly so when a section of the piece, cut out for analysis, was examined along the edge. This piece was marked "A" and submitted to H. F. Keller, Ph.D., Professor of Chemistry of the Boys' High School, Philadelphia, and long an expert in copper in the "Lake" regions of Michigan. The analysis of the plate marked "A" is subjoined:

"This metal is of extraordinary purity. Minute quantities of iron and silver are the only impurities distributed throughout its entire mass.

"Quantitative determinations yielded:

Silver . . . . 0.0022 per cent.
Iron . . . . 0.0272 " "

"In one part of the plate a very small proportion (0.0016 per cent.) of lead was also found, but this must be regarded as due to local contamination from an external source, for other parts of the same plate are absolutely free from lead. Other metals such as bismuth, antimony, arsenic, nickel, etc., are also entirely absent.

[1] The analysis should be made with the utmost care, bearing in mind that most of the sulphuric acid to be had in this country contains lead. Analyses made for us are duplicated to blank to guarantee absence of foreign matter from the chemicals employed.

"The plate is coated with oxide and carbonate of copper and in some places also with clay, and with oxide and phosphate of iron.

"The percentage of copper in the metallic portion of the plate was estimated to be 99.969 per cent."

Here we clearly have an ornament of native copper, of aboriginal make, used by the Indians along with objects obtained from the whites, just as in this mound we met with beads of shell and beads of glass together.

Just where this native copper came from, of course we cannot say. It may have come down the Coosa river from where some of De Soto's men saw highly-colored copper, undoubtedly native, a locality believed by Pickett[1] to be in the present De Kalb County, Alabama.

More likely it came from the "Lake" region of Michigan and worked its way southward in course of trade.

Another breast-piece from this mound, showing no lamination, was marked " B " and submitted to Doctor Keller who reports as follows :

"The quantitative analysis of the copper plate marked " B " resulted as follows :

Copper	97.425	per cent.
Silver	0.037	" "
Lead	1.082	" "
Bismuth . .	0.035	" "
Antimony	0.378	" "
Arsenic . .	0.071	" "
Iron . .	0.024	" "
Nickel	0.013	" "
Residue, O, Cl, etc. .	0.935	" "

In this case we have a copper loaded with impurities, among which is lead, evidently the product of an early smelting process—in a word, copper supplied to the aborigines by Europeans.

It is seldom we are able to give from one mound, native copper showing aboriginal methods of work and copper undoubtedly obtained by the aborigines from European sources.

BRASS.

Bells.—Two sheet-brass bells, resembling sleigh-bells, were found with one burial and one with another. We read that hawk-bells, small bells attached to the legs of falcons, brought over by Europeans, were popular among the aborigines, but the bells found in this mound, each about 1 inch in diameter, were, perhaps, too large for use in falconry. The upper part of a small but heavy brass bell was present with a burial.

Miscellaneous.—An object of brass, perhaps the base of a candlestick, also was met with.

[1] "The History of Alabama," p. 27.

IRON.

Five objects of iron, one the link of a chain, some others possibly spikes, were found with burials at all depths—even at the base of the mound.

SILVER.

An undecorated gorget of silver, roughly circular, 1.9 inches in diameter, lay near a burial.

GLASS.

Glass beads were present in five or six instances, some near the base.

DOG.

Close to the base was the skeleton of a dog, the skull of which, though the skeleton was of post-Columbian origin and possibly of mixed breed, was sent to Professor Putnam who is now engaged in a careful study of aboriginal dogs,[1] in the hope that it might prove useful for comparison.

The existence of a pre-Columbian dog is denied by no one.

Cabeça de Vaca on his long journey among the tribes before unseen by white men, repeatedly encountered dogs, as did the expedition under De Soto. Upon one occasion many dogs served as food for De Soto's men on the upper Coosa, a part of the Alabama river.

We have found skeletal remains of dogs in Florida shell-heaps[2] which are undoubtedly pre-Columbian and skeletons of dogs were present, singly, in certain mounds opened by us in Florida[3] and in South Carolina,[4] while in some of the Georgia sea-islands[5] man's truest friend was accorded a regular sepulture in the general burial mounds.

ASSOCIATION OF OBJECTS.

In a post-Columbian mound the association of objects with burials is of peculiar interest, showing the use of articles obtained from the whites along with objects of purely aboriginal origin. Not to weary the reader with too long a list we give a few examples.

With the skeleton of a child were two shell gorgets and two pins of shell.

With bones of an adult were: an undecorated gorget of shell; two fine shell pins; massive beads of shell; a flat, oblong shell bead with double perforation; and two glass beads.

A stone hatchet, shell beads and two copper pendants lay together, 8 feet down.

[1] "Thirty-second Annual Report Peabody Museum," page 4.

[2] "American Naturalist," July, 1892.

[3] "Certain Sand Mounds of the St. John's River, Florida." Part II. Journ. Acad. Nat. Sci. Phila., Vol. X, pg. 157. "Florida Coast Mounds North of the St. Johns River," pg. 28. Privately printed, Philadelphia, 1896.

[4] "Certain Aboriginal Mounds, Coast of South Carolina." Journ. Acad. Nat. Sci. Phila. Vol. XI, pg. 149.

[5] "Certain Aboriginal Mounds of the Georgia Coast." Journ. Acad. Nat. Sci. Phila., Vol. XI, pg. 127 et sal.

Five feet from the surface, with human remains, lay a brass bell, the brass base of a candlestick and shell beads.

Glass beads with a gorget and beads of shell had been placed with remains of a child. Near the base, together, lay a stone "celt," two discoidal stones, a bit of iron and a copper pendant.

A shell drinking cup, a stone "celt," sheet copper and iron lay together with human remains on the base.

Not far from the mound just described, was an undulation composed of midden refuse. No burials were met with in it.

In the same field was another rise in the ground, composed of dark sandy loam with many sherds and mussel-shells.

Lying on the surface, where the plough had thrown it out, was the central portion of the shaft of a human femur, 4.8 inches in length. At one extremity of the fragment was an interesting exhibition of workmanship, the end being reamed out almost to a cutting edge, probably to serve as the handle to a tool.

Careful search was made in the refuse heap, resulting in the finding, about 6 inches below the surface, of another fragment which fitted to the one already found, making a total length of 8 inches. This portion of the shaft of the femur, presumably a woman's, is the proximal part with the articular portion roughly broken off. The bone is highly polished, presumably through wear, and a part of the linea aspera is worked or worn away.

This interesting specimen is shown in Fig. 51, where it is represented as raised somewhat at one end and is consequently foreshortened.

During all our mound work we have but twice before found human bones bearing trace of workmanship.

In the Tick island mound was a piercing implement wrought from a human femur,[1] while from the mound at Bluffton came a part of a parietal bone decorated with incised lines, probably a portion of a gorget.

Professor Jeffries Wyman,[2] the pioneer of shell-heap investigation in Florida, says: "We have not found tools made of human bones, but it is not improbable that these were used for such purposes, as the sawed human thigh-bone found at Osceola mound naturally suggests." Professor Wyman, in a foot-note refers to a humerus from a human skeleton, ground and scraped as though for a tool, found in a shell-heap at Ipswich, Mass. Professor Putnam also has described this bone.

Fig. 51.—Human thigh-bone showing workmanship. Small mound on Charlotte Thompson Place. (Full size.)

[1] "Certain Sand Mounds of the St. Johns River, Florida," Part I.
[2] "Fresh-Water Shell Mounds of the St. Johns River, Florida," p. 51.

Three human bones covered with elaborate incised carving from Ohio mounds have been described by Professor Putnam and Mr. Willoughby, jointly, in the *Proceedings* of the American Association for the Advancement of Science, 1896, and we are indebted to Mr. Willoughby for the information that there are in the Peabody Museum fragments of two elaborately carved parietal bones from an altar in the famous Turner group of mounds, Ohio.

Less than half a mile in a westerly direction from the large mound is a mound about 4 feet high, of red clay, which had been so dug into previously that farther investigation was not considered advisable.

MOUND ON THE ROGERS PLACE, MONTGOMERY COUNTY.

About 1 mile in an easterly direction from the mound on the Charlotte Thompson Place is a considerably smaller mound, on the property of Mr. Loraine Rogers, of Montgomery, who kindly placed it at our disposition.

The mound was partially investigated by us, but as it seemed to be of a domiciliary character it was not extensively dug through.

MOUND NEAR HORSE-SHOE BEND, ELMORE COUNTY.

About 5 miles below Montgomery, on the right side of the river, going down, at the upper end of a bend known as the Horseshoe, in a cultivated field, about 100 yards from the river was a mound bearing no sign of previous examination. Its height was 4 feet 9 inches; its diameter of base, 40 feet. It was trenched in from the margin considerably beyond the center, with kind permission of Mr. Henry Irvin, of Montgomery, the owner.

It was of unstratified clay with no sign of sherds, fireplaces or bone, and was doubtless erected for domiciliary purposes.

MOUNDS IN THIRTY-ACRE FIELD, MONTGOMERY COUNTY.

At Big Eddy Landing, about one mile below the union of the Coosa and the Tallapoosa rivers, is the plantation of Mr. A. M. Baldwin, of Montgomery, through whose kindness and that of Mr. T. R. Stacey, of Chisholm, Ala., under whose care the plantation is, we were permitted to make full investigation.

The Thirty-Acre Field mound, in the midst of a cultivated field bordering the swamp, about one-half mile in an E. by S. direction from the Alabama river, had been at times washed by freshets, but still preserved the shape of an inverted bowl. Its height was 13 feet; its base diameter, 88 feet; the diameter of the summit plateau, 42 feet.

In order to determine the nature of the mound, about one-half the circumference, the eastern and the northern portions, were surrounded and excavation along the line of the base was carried in for about 10 feet without discovering interments.

Next a portion of the trench, about 26 feet across, was carried in 8 feet farther, or almost to the margin of the summit plateau, still with no trace of human remains

Then the mound was surrounded at a height of 7 feet from the base, where the section was 62 feet in diameter, and excavation along that level was begun. The first burial was met with 4.5 feet from the start, or about 5 feet outside the margin of the summit plateau, but not until we had gone considerably nearer to the plateau were burials in any number encountered.

It became evident from this and from the digging which preceded it, that the mound, which was made of small layers and considerable masses of sand with strata of clay blackened by fire and admixture of midden refuse, had been dwelt upon and then increased in height and diameter a number of times, and that, during the various periods of occupation of the mound, burials had been made by digging down from the surface of what happened to be the summit plateau at the time of the burial. For instance, burials were present, dug down from the level of the summit plateau as it was at the time of our investigation, while other burials lay considerably deeper in pits, which could be traced only as far as unbroken strata three or four feet above. Well in, toward the center was a grave 10 feet from the surface, but only 4 feet 2 inches beneath unbroken strata.

Our excavation, therefore, was concave in shape, the deepest portion being at the center of the mound. It is possible some burials were missed by us, but we believe them to have been few indeed.

Owing to a considerable number of burials in a comparatively restricted area there were, as may well be imagined, many aboriginal disturbances by digging of other graves.

Without considering such scattered bones, 111 skeletons were met with, all in anatomical order, some flexed to the right, some to the left. Others were partly flexed, that is to say, the trunks lay upon the back with the legs drawn up against the thighs and turned to the right or to the left.

Skeleton No. 102, adult, lay with the trunk on the back, the head pressed forward on the chest, upper arms along the body and forearms across the trunk. The legs were drawn up to the thighs, the knees to the thorax. The feet were turned inward toward each other, the toes meeting below the pelvis.

As this skeleton presented certain features of interest as to form of interment and was in much better condition than most others in the mound, it was decided to make an effort to save it intact. The clay, except that immediately under the bones, was dug away until the skeleton lay a couple of feet above the general level of that part of the excavation.

Next, the skeleton and the bed of supporting clay were saturated with glue and a slow fire was built around to aid in drying. This fire was kept up about six hours.

Then the skeleton and the mass beneath were allowed twenty-four hours for additional solidification, a platform having been built above to keep off dew and rain.

The next step was to sever the skeleton with about one foot of partially dried

Fig. 24.—Burial No. 102. Heaped in Older Area Field. Not to scale.

clay from the rest of the mass, with the aid of a large saw, and clay and bones, supported by the saw, were gently pushed over on to a sort of stretcher constructed for the purpose in advance.

The mass, by no means light, was carried by men long used to mound work, across the field and down a slippery clay bank to a bateau in which the journey was safely made to our steamer lying in the river.

After this, the mass was treated to another bath of glue and allowed to remain two weeks on the boiler of the steamer. The next stage was reached in our laboratory on the upper deck where all the clay, but a thin layer, was worked off and two iron rods were placed longitudinally beneath. The base of the clay then received a coat of cement which included the rods.

The mass was carefully packed in a crate and the crate, in its turn, encased in a box, surrounded by elastic packing, and the whole was sent North by express under special arrangement as to care in transportation.

This burial is shown in Fig. 52.

A few skeletons of infants lay apparently at full length.

The skeletons in this mound headed in all directions.

The bones, which were badly decayed, no cranium with the exception of that of Burial No. 102 being preserved, showed no fractures during life and in but one case, osteitis, was a pathological condition present.

SHELL.

Beads.—With a considerable number of skeletons were beads of shell, usually at the neck, but at times extending down the chest and occasionally at the wrist. Some were small marine shells (*Marginella*) pierced for stringing; others were of the ordinary type, of various sizes, including sections of columellæ, 2.3 inches in major diameter.

Fig. 53.—Gorget of shell. Mound in Thirty-Acre Field. (Full size.)

Fig. 54.—Drawing of gorget shown in Fig. 53. (Full size.)

With one skeleton were forty-eight flat beads, almost square, as a rule, with double perforation, somewhat larger, but less ornate than those from Durand's Bend and from the Charlotte Thompson Place.

Pins.—Quantities of shell pins, some 6.5 inches in length, were with the skeletons, always near the skull. No less than six were found with a single burial.

Gorgets.—Near the bones of an adult and of an infant, buried together, was a circular gorget of shell, 2 inches in diameter, slightly broken at one part of the rim. The decoration is carved and engraved on one side, as shown in Fig. 55, where the figure is reversed, and shows a grotesque head probably represented as wearing a mask, with a great nose and a huge, protruding tongue. The design on this gorget has been carefully drawn to scale, much enlarged by the aid of a magnifying glass, and reduced to natural size in reproduction. The excised portions are shown in black. Prof. Frank Hamilton Cushing believes the figure to be kneeling, one hand grasping a baton, the other resting on the exceedingly flexed knee. The teeth are closed. The figure is probably represented as blowing or hissing. According to Professor Cushing the figure has the double headed forelock common to certain warrior figures on shell gorgets and copper plates.

In General Thruston's "Antiquities of Tennessee," Second Edition, Chapter IX, and supplement to Chapter IX, is a comprehensive account, fully illustrated, of these rare and interesting human figures sometimes found on gorgets of shell and plates of copper, and they are also described in Professor Holmes' "Art in Shell." [1]

With skeleton No. 66, a child's, was an oblong gorget of shell with rounded corners, having double perforation for suspension at one corner, 1.8 inches by 1.6 inches. In the center is an incised circle with semi-perforations and a quarter circle with a semi-perforation in each corner, as shown in Fig. 54.

FIG. 54.—Gorget of shell. Mound in Thirty-Acre Field. (Full size.)

FIG. 55.—Gorget of shell. Mound in Thirty-Acre Field. (Full size.)

Skeleton No. 90, of an infant, had two hairpins of shell and two circular gorgets of shell. Curiously enough, no beads were met with.

One gorget, 2 inches in diameter, has on one side an interesting incised decoration representing two birds, standing, facing each other, their bills almost in contact (Fig. 55).

[1] Second Annual Report, Bureau of Ethnology, 1880–1881.

Fig. 56.—Gorget of shell. Mound in Thirty-Acre
Field. (Full size.)

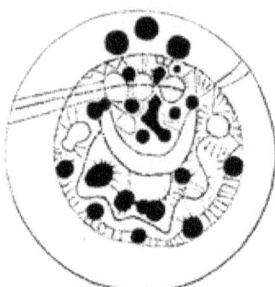

Fig. 56a.—Drawing of gorget shown in Fig. 56.
(Full size.)

Fig. 57.—Earthenware vessel. Mound in Thirty-Acre Field. (About five-sixths size.)

The other gorget, freshly perforated for suspension, shown in halftone, Fig. 56, where the figures have unfortunately been reversed, and drawn in Fig. 56a, has a design we have been unable to decipher.

Professor Cushing, who has kindly given the matter of these gorgets considerable attention, considers the design to be figures of blowing gods or warriors surrounded by one of the typical gorget serpents.

Several other gorgets, all undecorated, broken beyond redemption, were met with.

Miscellaneous.—With a number of massive beads was an ovoid object of shell, imperforate, 1.9 inches long by about 1.4 inches in thickness.

EARTHENWARE

Vessels.—With burial No. 54 was a vessel of the type in use at Durand's Bend though much smaller and having, in addition to the upright ridges, the small loop-shaped handles. This vessel has a maximum diameter of 4.3 inches and is 2.8 inches in height. It was unfortunately broken by a blow from a spade, but has been partly pieced together. With another burial was a water-bottle with maximum diameter of 4.9 inches and a height of 4.2 inches having five protuberances around the body, enclosed in double incised lines. Between are incised lines running diagonally. The vessel had fallen to pieces, but had been put together with the exception of a portion of the base (Fig. 57).

Fig. 58.—Tobacco-pipe. Mound in Thirty-Acre Field. (Full size.)   Fig. 59.—Handle of earthenware vessel. Mound in Thirty-Acre Field. (Full size.)

Tobacco-pipe.—An undecorated tobacco-pipe was found in loose dirt thrown out by the diggers (Fig. 58).

Miscellaneous.—Loose in the mound, in midden refuse, were numbers of earthenware discs, wrought from sherds, for use in games as before described.

The earthenware head of a bird, which had seen service as the handle of a vessel, was found loose in the earth (Fig. 59).

STONE

Tobacco-pipe.—In earth thrown out by the diggers was a rude soapstone pipe with oblong bowl, similar in type to those described by us in other reports as coming from the lower St. Johns river, Florida, though smaller.

"*Hoe-shaped Implements.*"—Burial No. 79, adult, a delicate male or a female, had shell beads at the neck and a "hoe-shaped implement" of volcanic rock, 5.5 inches long and 4.5 inches in maximum diameter of blade. There is no perforation. No mark of use is apparent.

Burial No. 88, adult, had shell beads and hairpins and an imperforate "hoe-shaped implement" of volcanic rock, 6.3 inches long and 4.8 inches across the body. It also bears no mark of use.

With burial No. 105, an adult, was an interesting association of objects. By the neck were massive beads of shell and an ovoid object of shell. On the chest lay a "hoe-shaped implement" of felsitic rock, with a shank unusually long, the total length being 9.4 inches, while the maximum diameter of blade is but 4.5 inches. On one side of the shank are marks where a perforation has been attempted with a tubular drill. A handle has encircled part of the shank beginning at the abandoned perforation and extending back to about 4.5 inches from the end, as may be seen in Fig. 60.

Discoidal Stones.—Throughout the mound, in midden refuse, were a number of flat pebbles rudely rounded for use as discoidal stones.

At the elbow of Burial No. 45 was a beautifully wrought discoidal stone of quartz, 3 inches in diameter, while near the head of Burial No. 100 was a slightly larger discoidal stone of *Granulyte*. Several smaller discoidals of volcanic rock came from this mound. A discoidal of clayey rock bore an incised cross (Fig. 61).

"*Celts.*"—Several hatchets and chisels of the usual rocks were present in the mound.

Miscellaneous.—Scattered throughout the mound, but never with burials, were numbers of perforated pebbles, natural formations, to which we have already alluded.

Fig. 61.—Disc of clayey rock. Mound on Thorn's Neck Field. (Full size.)

Several unassociated arrowheads were met with and one of quartz near the head of a skeleton.

Fragments of mica were encountered in places.

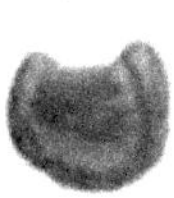

Fig. 62.—Ornament of red jasper. Mound on Thorn's Neck Field. (Full size.)

Near skeletons were a small bowl seemingly made from part of a geode and a beautiful little ornament of red jasper, perforated for suspension (Fig. 62).

COPPER.

Two discs of sheet copper were in disturbed earth near a skeleton, while two other skeletons had discs of a similar type on either side of the skull. These ornaments, one pair of which was 2 inches in diameter each, the other 1.5 inches each, were of the familiar type, namely, an incised boss in the middle with a small central perforation for attachment and marginal decoration of concavo-convex beading. All apparently had been mounted on a thin layer of wood.

With a skeleton were the remains of a sheet copper pendant in the shape of an arrowhead with blunt point.

MISCELLANEOUS.

A rattle consisting of a tortoise shell, much decayed, containing many small pebbles, lay near a skeleton, and near another was a piercing implement of bone pointed at either end.

REMARKS.

Nothing indicating a knowledge of the whites was met with in this interesting mound with a single exception. A colored man at work at a place across which much superficial material had been thrown, found a leaden bullet. We do not consider this discovery as of necessity indicating a post-Columbian origin for the mound, and are inclined to believe that aborigines having a leaden bullet would have had many other articles of European make which would have found their way into the body of the mound.

SMALLER MOUND IN THE THIRTY-ACRE FIELD, MONTGOMERY COUNTY.

About twenty-five yards in a westerly direction from the mound in the Thirty-Acre Field, was a much smaller one almost ploughed away. In fact, had it not been of a lighter color than the surrounding soil, it might have escaped our notice. Its height was about 1 foot; its diameter, about 50 feet.

It was completely dug through at a depth of about 1 to 1.5 feet from the surface where undisturbed clay was met with. The upper part of the mound was of yellowish clay; the lower, of dark material consisting of clay and of midden refuse.

Thirty-one interments, similar to those found in the other mound, were uncovered.

In the debris were the usual pebbles, chipped into discoidal form, polished chisels, broken "celts," hammer-stones, etc. Also a perforated disc of earthenware and another with the perforation surrounded by lines, as shown in Fig. 63.

FIG. 63.—Disc of earthenware. Smaller mound in Thirty-Acre Field. (Full size.)

With the burials were many shell pins and beads including a considerable number of flat beads larger than those found before. We give a selection in Fig. 64.

In addition, were a handsome discoidal stone; a stopper-shaped object of earthenware, somewhat broken; four cubes of galena; a sheet copper pendant, badly broken, similar in style to the one from the other mound and to those from the Charlotte Thompson Place.

With burials were two lots of sheet copper pendants of the prevalent blunt-pointed arrowhead type. The first lot of seven varied in length from 2.8 inches to 3.9 inches and in maximum breadth from 1 inch to 1.8 inches. Two lay separately near the head, while five, near by, piled one upon the other, were apparently upon decayed bark enclosed in matting which the copper salt had preserved. This matting was made of split cane which, in one direction, goes once under and four times over and, on the same side, in the other direction, runs over one and under four, as shown in Fig. 65. On the opposite side of the matting the pattern is, of course, reversed.

Fig. 64.—Shell beads. Smaller mound in Thirty-Acre Field. (Full size.)

The other lot of pendants, eight in number, were piled one upon the other. In size they resembled the others.

The decoration on all the pendants had been conferred by pressure. On the

Fig. 65.—Matting. Smaller mound in Thirty-Acre Field. (Full size.)

upper part was a portion of the aboriginal eye, and as this eye was not complete, it seemed to us at first as though the pendants had been cut from a sheet of copper previously decorated. Upon closer examination, however, it was noted that the section

FIG. 66.—Pendants of sheet copper. Smaller mound in Thirty-Acre Field. (Full size.)

FIG. 67.—Pendants of sheet copper. Smaller mound in Thirty-Acre Field. (Full size.)

of the eye always occupied the same place on the pendant, and that the eyes, though having a general resemblance, were in no case exactly alike. Moreover, the decoration beneath, though similar in a general way, was never identical as would have been the case, had the design resulted from a stamp rather than from the pressure of a moving object such as horn pushed down on copper placed over buckskin. We have not been able to learn the meaning of this design which, however, is distinctly aboriginal. A selection of these interesting pendants is shown in Figs. 66, 67.

There came also from this mound a small, coarse, undecorated pot and a water-bottle of smooth black ware, badly broken, 5 inches high and 4.5 inches in maximum diameter, with incised decoration (Fig. 68).

MOUND IN BIG EDDY FIELD, MONTGOMERY COUNTY.

This mound, in a field known as Big Field or the Big Eddy Field, is about one-half mile in a southwesterly direction from the larger mound in the Thirty-Acre Field and is under the same ownership. In the midst of a level field, long under cultivation, it is a great landmark looming up from all directions. Though washed by rain and by freshets it has fairly well retained its shape of a truncated cone, and has been a place of refuge for stock when territory for miles around had been submerged. Its height was 16 feet 7 inches; the diameter of its base, 108 feet, and that of the summit plateau, about 50 feet.

FIG. 88.—Water bottle of earthenware. Summit mound in Thirty-Acre Field.   (Full size.)

Owing to its advantage in flood time a great reduction in the height of the mound was not deemed advisable. We were, however, permitted to dig through the upper 6 feet.

The mound, so far as investigated, was of much softer material than the mound in the Thirty-Acre Field, being homogeneous, composed of sandy clay, without layers of occupation, though midden refuse and marks of fire were present in places.

It transpired during the digging that the upper part of the mound had been in use as a sort of cemetery in comparatively recent times. Curiously enough, as though a survival of the aboriginal custom of placing objects with the dead, on the breast of a child in a pine coffin was a Spanish piece of eight reals of the year 1815—one of those "pieces of eight" which the buccaneers so highly prized.

In all, nineteen aboriginal burials, some greatly disturbed, were met with, the form coinciding with that in vogue in the mounds in the Thirty-Acre Field. All bones were past preservation, through decay.

With burials were a handsome "celt" of fine-grained *Syenite*, 14.5 inches in length; a chisel; quantities of shell beads and pins; a mushroom-shaped object of earthenware, somewhat broken; a deposit of copper pendants, in small pieces, of the type already described; two discs of copper of the type found in the Thirty-Acre Field mound and another deposit of pendants, one on the other, similar in type to the other lot. These pendants lay on a coarse fabric of twisted vegetable fibre, which, in its turn, lay upon cane matting. This material, like other wrapping material found on copper in other sections, was, in our opinion, not to envelop the copper alone, but was simply a part of a general envelopment of the entire skeleton of which the portion found, preserved by the copper salt, alone remains. We see how the Peruvians wrapped their dead and doubtless, in many sections, a similar custom obtained in this country.

Mr. Harlan I. Smith, of the Jesup North Pacific Expedition, has recently published the results of his work in the southern interior of British Columbia.[1] Of the burials there he tells us, "the bodies were buried upon the side, with the knees drawn up to the chest. They were wrapped in a fabric made of sage-brush bark, and were covered with mats of woven rushes."

MOUND AT JACKSON'S BEND, ELMORE COUNTY.

Jackson's Bend, having the Alabama on one side, the Coosa on another, has, on the Coosa side, a farm belonging to Mr. Brown Jackson, colored, overlooking the water. In periods succeeding floods it has been the custom of those residing near

Fig. 69.—Part of tobacco-pipe. Jackson's Bend. (Full size.)

to examine the section of the bluff laid bare and to dig where dark-colored earth, running down, indicated the presence of a grave. We were shown many objects of interest taken from these graves, some of which, kindly presented to us, showed contact with the whites. Among the objects of aboriginal make was a portion of a bowl of a tobacco-pipe in the shape of a human head (Fig. 69).

In the S. E. corner of the Bluff Field, over which were scattered numerous arrowheads of quartz and of chert, was a mound long under cultivation, about 3.5 feet high and of indeterminable basal diameter. This mound, which, we are told, had been previously dug into, was trenched to a certain extent by us, resulting in the discovery of the head and shoulders of a skeleton with a number of marine shells (*Oliva literata*) perforated longitudinally for stringing. The remainder of

[1] "Science," N. S., Vol. IX, No. 224, pp. 535 to 539, April 14, 1899.

the skeleton, presumably, had been dug away. Not far distant, near the surface, lay a skeleton on its back with machine-made nails in association—doubtless a recent burial.

GENERAL REMARKS.

As we have seen, the mounds of the Alabama are small in size, increasing somewhat in the northern portion where the country is more elevated, and present no striking features structurally.

Of sites of former cemeteries reported to us in considerable number, revealed by the action of floods, but one still yielded interments to a careful search, so, as to these, we are unable to draw definite conclusions.

The artifacts of the early inhabitants of the banks of the Alabama resemble in a general way aboriginal objects used elsewhere. Quartz largely superseded, as a material for projectile points, the chert in use in Florida and on the Georgia coast. Earthenware was often of fairly good quality and, as a rule, had admixture of pounded shell with the clay. The type and decoration of vessels found entire by us were not striking, though heads of birds and other fragments occasionally found indicate the use of such articles as handles on interesting forms of ware, and with the admixture of pounded shell and with loop-shaped handles suggest Tennessean influence, while occasional polished black ware recalls the vessels of Mississippi. The gritty ware of lower Georgia and its complicated stamp decoration were almost absent from the Alabama river, though occasional sherds with decoration of the kind prevailing in Georgia, Carolina, and sometimes found in upper Florida were met with. No pottery was found of the highest standard of that beautiful ware in use along the Gulf in aboriginal times.

Perforation below the rim on opposite sides of the vessel, which served for purposes of suspension, was practically absent from vessels found by us along the Alabama river.

The most striking feature of the Alabama, and one new to our work, was plural burials of uncremated bones in single urns. On the Georgia coast, while vessels often filled to the top with calcined remains are met with, we have never found, or heard of the finding of, over one unburnt skeleton in a single vessel.

Another feature of interest was the almost total absence of cremation. While in Florida this rite was often practiced, and while the mounds of many of the rivers of Georgia and of its coast teem with calcined human remains contained in urns or unenclosed, but one case of cremation was met with by us along the entire Alabama river.

INDEX.

www.ingramcontent.com/pod-product-compliance
Lightning Source LLC
Chambersburg PA
CBHW021631270326
41931CB00008B/969